DARK

PSYCHOLOGY

AND

GASLIGHTING

MANIPULATION

Advanced Methods to Master Dark Psychology,
Mind Control, Persuasion, and Ways to Identify
and avoid Gaslighting Manipulators

MELINDA XAVIER

Table of Contents

Introduction

Dark psychology and gaslighting manipulation are common forms of behavior primarily used to exert control over people. This comprehensive beginner's guide aims to give you, the reader, an in-depth look at these types of behaviors and help you to learn simple and effective techniques to either influence human behavior, learn how to use it, or recognize it when it happens to you. If you can recognize it and do it yourself, you'll be able to avoid the abuse that results from it.

The purpose of this book is to give the reader insight into dark psychology and manipulation traits. Among the different methods used to control other people are lying by omission, projecting blame on others, denial, covert intimidation, shaming, evasion, and brandishing anger. The purpose is to destroy people's self-esteem and cause confusion. Once the manipulators achieve this goal, they can set the agenda and become self-styled group leaders.

This book is different from other similar books on the market in that it's easy to understand. The subjects of dark psychology and gaslighting manipulation are usually challenging to understand. However, they are presented in a simple way such that you can understand them without seeking help from other individuals with knowledge in this area.

It's a great book for beginners because it explains all the basics you should know about this subject simply and concisely. It highlights all the terms and concepts involved in this subject. It explains all the elements involved in dark psychology and why people use it both for good and bad intentions. If you are a beginner interested in learning about this topic, this book is for you.

In most cases, the desire to influence other people and control their behavior is caused by a love of power. It provides hands-on instructions on the measures you can take to protect yourself from someone trying to use dark psychology and manipulation to control you.

The manipulators are specifically concerned about exercising total power over certain people, but the good thing about this book is that it helps you keep them at bay. When you read the entire book, you will learn different measures you can take to overcome the fear of dealing with dark psychology.

You will also gain confidence when dealing with people who are obsessed with influencing or controlling other individuals to follow them. More importantly, you'll become the master of your destiny once you are equipped with the different strategies you get from this book to protect yourself from manipulators.

Chapter 1

What Is Persuasion?

Persuasion is one of the most influential psychological skills you can develop when learning dark psychology. Whether you want to become a successful leader in the business world or society or simply want to learn how to make your point, mastering the art of persuasion will open many doors for you. It comes with positive influencing skills and many other benefits - for you and those around you.

Despite popular belief, persuasion is not about making people do something they don't want to or shouldn't do; it's more about helping them realize the advantages of doing something they would do anyway but weren't sure if it was the right decision. Of course, your assistance is based on convincing them to see and agree with your point of view, but this only helps establish a clear line of communication. When you have assertive persuasion skills, you can present convincing arguments and facts.

The power of this skill lies in the subtlety of the messages. Whether they are sent verbally, nonverbally, or through the media, persuasive messages are rarely overt and often only symbolic. Understanding how persuasion works can help you become more aware of the influence of these messages - and will also teach you how to use your skill more effectively.

When and Why Is Persuasion Used?

Persuasion is a skill that can be used for a variety of purposes. Some situations when persuasive messages can be helpful are:

- **Marketing:** Media, visual, and written advertisements can all be fueled by the power of persuasion.

- **Converting Leads to Sales:** Potential customers are drawn in and persuaded to make a purchase. Then, they can also be influenced to remain loyal customers.

- **Motivational Pieces:** When writing a motivational article, delivering a speech, or creating any other persuasive content, your motivational messages will influence people.

- **Encouraging Positive Academic Decisions:** Teachers, counselors, mentors, and even parents persuade students to engage in learning towards better career options in the future.

- **Awareness Campaigns:** Sustainability, diversity, and health awareness are just some of the common areas which use persuasion techniques to bring awareness to broad audiences. Whatever method a persuader uses to get their point across, they'll always promote ideas that align with their values - and with which they want others to align.

- **Employee Motivation:** Team leaders and employers persuade their teams to work effectively by motivating them with the promise of a reward.

- **Deals and Negotiations**: Business owners often use persuasion to cement lucrative business deals and safeguard their capital and interests.

Since persuasion is a skill that can be developed and honed, it can be used for many more purposes than just those described above. As long as you can assess your audience's needs, establish communication, learn the advantages that can be gained, see how to counter objections, and find common ground, you'll be able to send a persuasive message.

How Persuasion Is Done

Persuasion can be achieved in numerous ways, but most techniques rely on a few fundamental principles. Using these principles appropriately can make any message more persuasive, influential, and, more importantly, successful. Depending on the outcome you want, you can apply these principles separately or combine them.

Reciprocity

Most people are more likely to do something for someone else if they know they can expect to be paid back. For example, online marketers often ask people to provide their email addresses to receive future notifications about their products and services. They also offer to send coupons or discounts on goods, persuading potential buyers to provide their email addresses willingly.

Similarly, if you want to ask a friend for a favor, promising or doing a similar favor for them can make it easier to persuade them.

Fear of Missing Out

People can be persuaded to change their thoughts and behavior easily if you convince them that by not doing so, they could miss out on something important. Hinting that people will lose access to a product or service which is only available for only a limited period or presenting evidence of scarcity is just some of the techniques used in applying this principle. The perfect example of this is booking travel and accommodation online - there are always just a few rooms left in the hotel you are considering.

The Appeal of Authority

If someone believes that you are an expert on whatever topic you are talking about, they'll be more likely to be persuaded by your message. This is why authority figures like scientists, doctors, politicians, and members of law enforcement are held in high esteem by society. This phenomenon goes hand in hand with compliance - the more important someone is, the more likely people are to comply with their wishes. However, if you can sound authoritative and project an air of being an expert, you'll be able to persuade people to do your will or change their minds to your way of thinking.

Consistency and Commitment

Once someone makes a decision about their behavior, they continue with it until they are persuaded to do otherwise. Commitment creates consistency, which is hard to change. To do it, you must make people commit to whatever you want them to do. For example, if you want to ask a friend to start exercising with you, you'll need to persuade them to commit. Ask them to call if they need to miss a session for whatever reason. This way, they'll stay committed and join you consistently in your exercise sessions.

The Need for Social Proof

People often make life decisions based on what their family, friends, or peers do. It is natural to think that if everyone else around us chooses to express the same behavior, then it must be the safest one. We buy similar or identical things our friends do, support the same beliefs, and agree with the same persuasive messages our friends do. To persuade one person, you'll need to influence everyone else around them. Once they see everyone else adopting your point of view, they'll follow suit as well.

Like and Dislike

People are more likely to agree with someone's argument if they like them or at least know them well enough to decide whether they could like them. On the other hand, if they don't know or like the person, they will not be interested in their message. This is a deeper version of the social proof principle, as not all decisions can be made simply by observing others around you. To make some of the most critical decisions in your life, you'll need to be influenced by a person with whom you have a good relationship.

What You Need to Become a Better Persuader

Here are some skills that can help you improve your persuasion skills:

Interpersonal Skills

Interpersonal skills help you feel more confident and comfortable when interacting with others. Strong interpersonal skills make it easier to initiate a conversation and establish a connection with your conversation partner. Both are skills required if you want to persuade anyone to agree with your point of view. To improve this skill, watch how other people interact with each other in a similar setting. Whether it's a workplace or a social setting, there are always unwritten rules to follow if you want to interact with people. After noting the qualities that facilitated other people's interactions, you can then think about how to improve your own. You can also practice the skills you want to get better at by engaging with people you are already close to, as interacting with them will be easier and enable you to deepen your interpersonal skills.

Communication Style

A good communication style goes a long way in coming up with persuasive arguments. To achieve this, practice sharing your ideas by using a language everyone will understand. Use simple words and be as concise as possible. Remember, people generally have a short attention span and will only focus on your message for a brief period. Communication also includes gestures, tone of voice, body language, and facial expressions when speaking to people. You want all these nonverbal clues to align with the persuasive arguments you are trying to make in the shortest time possible.

Deductive Reasoning

Deductive reasoning skills are a great tool for making your messages more persuasive. Analyze the situation surrounding your arguments. Think about which solution would sound the most logical to a listener, and only then offer an insight. To sound more knowledgeable and credible, you can also research the topic before even beginning your argument. This way, you will collect all the critical facts necessary to provide a persuasive viewpoint. Engaging in creative activities and other problem-solving behaviors may also strengthen your logical thinking capabilities.

Emotional Intelligence

Emotional intelligence refers to how much awareness you have of your own and the feelings of others. Emotionally intelligent people can easily relate to others, interpret their feelings, and establish trust. All this makes sending persuasive messages more personal and effective. This is another skill you can develop by observing how others interact with you. Emotions are often expressed as nonverbal cues, like body language. For example, you can easily tell whether someone is engaged in conversation based on their body language alone. If someone crosses their arms, turns slightly away, and keeps glancing around during a conversation, they are probably not interested in conversing with you. This may be because of your own body posture or tone of voice, and modifying this can help you align with their emotions. Or, you may need to change the subject to something that the person you are talking to feels more comfortable about. Attempting to understand how they may feel will get you closer to persuading them.

Negotiation Techniques

Learning how to negotiate is a great way to ensure you'll reach a compromise every time you try persuading people to accept your opinion. Negotiation skills and strategies can be used in all types of conversations. You can use them to identify other people's values, needs, and desires and tell them how they can benefit from agreeing with your point. Knowing all this can help you develop more persuasive arguments, so the promise of agreement sounds more appealing. It's also helpful if you are willing to provide an alternative solution in case people don't agree with the first offer of agreement.

Active Listening Skills

Actively listening to what other people are saying to you in conversation will also help you develop persuasive arguments. You'll always be able to find some common ground with someone if you just listen closely. After that, all it takes is to incorporate this into your dialogue, and you'll already start to gain their trust. It'll make it more appealing for them to listen to your motivations and values. Allowing the other party to share their point of view without interruption also goes a long way in building effective communication. It'll allow you to understand what motivates your conversation partner, show them that you respect their opinion, or simply make them feel heard. Make sure to include nonverbal gestures like nodding in agreement as well.

The Effects of Persuasion

The effects of persuasion depend on the beliefs people form based on the persuasive arguments they hear. How they feel about the message also matters because emotions are also rationalized into ideas and beliefs. Here are some of the most common effects persuasion has on a listener.

It Changes Mood by Distracting

Persuasive messages distract people from their own thoughts, beliefs, and behaviors. When this happens, their mood will start affecting their attitude, allowing you to change it to work in your favor. The person you are influencing may realize their mood has changed, but they won't see how this change is relevant to their decision. Without persuasion, a person will always be able to consider their mood and its relevance to their behavior. Or, they'll give no thought to their feelings, not allowing them to shape their attitude.

It Affects Motivation

Whether someone can be persuaded depends on their motivation for self-defense and their ability to be accurate. No one likes their ideas to be countered by what they perceive to be pointless arguments. However, when persuaded by logical messages, they may see that their beliefs aren't accurate. By presenting accurate information,

argument, the others have already voiced their knowledge, making them confident they have been heard. Even if you counter their opinion with logical arguments, they'll know you value their impact and will remember it for future conversations.

It Leaves a Strong Impression

People's personal impressions of you have a powerful impact on your ability to persuade them. When you manage to influence them positively once, people will form a favorable impression of you. This will allow you to send more persuasive messages in the future. If you failed to leave an impression, you probably weren't successful in persuading them to align with your ideas and values at the outset. People always remember the source more than the argument. Persuasion can make you seem charismatic and knowledgeable, and people will remember you.

It Helps Decide the Nature of the Experience

People often aren't sure whether their experience was physical or mental, which means they probably can't decide how to act on it. To distinguish between the two different experiences, people turn to others who had the same experience for validation. They may even ask others without similar experiences (close friends and family) for their opinion. Either way, if someone asks your opinion about their experience, you can persuade them to see the situation as you've perceived it. Whether you consider it a physical or mental experience, persuasive arguments will help others decide as well.

The Benefits of Persuasion and Positive Influencing Skills

Despite all the misconceptions surrounding it, persuasion comes with several benefits. Here are some of the most common ones.

Improves Self-Expression

Developing strong persuasion skills can help you express yourself better. Because logical arguments are based on facts, other people are more likely to agree with them. Having your message validated in this way will build your self-esteem. Even if you start by stating your opinion, underlining it with valid proof from having studied the subject will give you more authority. Persuasion helps you make your thoughts heard by using facts to show other people's opinions are wrong. The more you practice this, the more confident you'll become in expressing your beliefs and ideas.

Makes You More Considerate

The key to effective persuasion is simply being honest. As mentioned before, a persuader will never try to manipulate their listener to accept their opinion. Instead, they'll provide facts that support their argument. When the listener applies these facts to their own thought processes, they'll be persuaded to agree. This means that to be persuasive, you also have to be considerate. Learning to influence others will teach you to always consider other people's ideas and feelings, no matter how different they may be from yours. You'll also try not to present false information because if found out, it leads to mistrust and may hurt other people's feelings.

Strengthens Relationships

Communication within relationships requires a lot of effort. Through persuasion, you can become more communication savvy, which, in turn, will also improve your relationship dynamics. In most cases, you'll reach listeners with facts and logic. They'll analyze the facts on their own and will see that your arguments are valid, leading to long-standing mutual understanding in the relationship. Or, you may assume that others are listening to your message only on an emotional level. In this case, they won't analyze the situation. You'll have to show them that you already did this and what your analysis uncovered. Once again, as soon as they see that you are right, understanding follows, and the relationships will endure.

Helps Overcome Resistance

Habits play a crucial role in the effectiveness of persuasion. Resistance to changing a habit is one of the most challenging factors standing against persuasive arguments. Effective persuasion should make others feel comfortable with changing their habit of listening to their own ideas. As you have seen in this chapter, one of the feelings of persuasion relies on empathy. If you show a person that you empathize with their difficulty in breaking a habit, you'll overcome their resistance, and they'll be persuaded.

Chapter 2

Methods of Persuasion

Now that you've learned what persuasion is and what makes it work, you can delve into specific persuasive techniques you can use to get your point across. This chapter discusses several helpful strategies to take your persuasion skills to the next level. From the most successful methods used by the media to more simple approaches, even beginners can take advantage of it - everyone can find a strategy that aligns with what they want to achieve.

Usage of Force

While persuasion is all about using the power of the mind rather than physical power to convince someone, this doesn't mean you can get your "foot in the door." In fact, this is a common approach, often recommended to beginners because of how easy it is to put into practice. It starts by getting someone to agree on a smaller point. When they do, you follow up by asking them to accept something bigger - usually an idea they have strong feelings against. By getting people to agree to the initial request, you are forcing them to set aside their beliefs, making it more likely to comply with the second request. Marketers use this method to encourage customers to buy products and services they can sample before purchasing. You can also use it to get friends to agree to a small favor, and once they do, you'll follow up with a more significant favor. They'll see no point in refusing you as they've already agreed to do something beforehand, so they might as well comply with the second request. In fact, they may even feel obligated to agree to the second request.

Creating a Need

Creating a need is another powerful tool used in persuasion. This method is based on establishing a need for basic and social aspects of life, such as shelter, self-esteem, love, and self-empowerment. It may also appeal to people's desire to be more popular and distinctive than others or, conversely, to become more similar to someone. Since most of these needs already exist, bringing them to the fore is a straightforward way to ensure they get attention. Once the desire is there, all the persuader needs to do is appeal to it.

Some of the ways this method can be practiced include selling items that promise to make you more like a well-respected or highly admired person. You can also look for a need that's already present in people's minds and appeal to it. Nothing helps you convince your friends to help you out more than complimenting them on their accomplishments. It makes them happy and self-realized and opens the door for you.

Using Illustrations and Words

Using loaded words and images is also a common persuasive technique. This usually goes hand in hand with appealing to people's needs. The images and words being used in this technique are designed to appeal to people's desires. For example, if you want to convince someone to start using organic products, you'll use words like "all-natural." You can also show research and images illustrating the benefits of the product. "New and improved" is another phrase often used to give more importance to an item, event, or situation. In this case, the words are underlined with high-resolution images shot under bright lighting and other special effects, showcasing the "newness" of the item.

Media and Advertisement Tricks

While the previous persuasion techniques can also be applied in marketing, advertising and media agencies have far more tricks up their sleeves. Here are some of the most common ones.

The Peak-End-Rule

Developed by a Nobel prize winner psychologist in the 1930s, the peak-end rule is one of the oldest marketing tools to rely on persuasion. According to this rule, if you have a peak at the end of your experience, you'll walk away with a more positive attitude. As opposed to not having a peak, but possibly a bad time, and most likely ending up disappointed and wishing you'd never have to repeat the experience again. The principle of this approach is that to persuade someone to adopt your attitude, you must ensure they have a good peak experience. They'll probably forget the rest of the experience - but will remember the end, which was seemingly beneficial for them. This is why marketing campaigns always culminate in one tumultuous experience at the end, promising the ultimate reward for customers willing to follow the entire campaign. It also ensures that most customers decide to follow any subsequent advertisements, hoping for another significant peak.

The Barnum Effect

The Barnum effect refers to people's tendency to accept vague depictions of a person, even though this description could be applied to almost every person on the planet. Since this also translates to statements about items and situations, marketers use it to present products and services to target audiences. The more generalized the messages are, the more they allow marketing agencies to find broader audiences. They can immediately connect with any individual from a large group. Individuals are more likely to listen if they think the message concerns them and can identify with the person presenting the product or service. Once this belief is created, the persuader can proceed with sending even more persuasive messages. Of course, the more honest the statements are, the easier it is to get people hooked.

Presenting Fear and Relief

Political campaigns are often based on the fear-and-relief theory. Candidates create fear about something at the beginning of their campaign, only to offer relief immediately after it. Their intention is to scare voters into thinking the only way to avoid a disaster is to choose them, while voting for the opposition may result in making the situation even worse. Campaigns creating fear around health issues and screenings also use a similar approach.

Offering Incentives

Using incentives like discounts, coupons, bundles, and other gifts is a popular way to attract visitors to a website. Many websites selling products or services use this method, persuading their visitors to make a purchase and return for more. These incentives unconsciously influence the behavior of website visitors, who decide on a purchase based on how attractive the offer is. Apart from saving money and discounts, other incentives may be cashback, free shipping and delivery, a buy one, get one free deal, and more. Other companies may offer slightly different incentives, such as an honor, the ability to show something to others, or the opportunity to help out others in need.

Using Decoys

Using an expensive or otherwise unattractive item as a decoy can greatly impact buyers' decision-making capabilities. Expensive items are always slow to sell in any product group - mostly because people love to save money. So, if they see an item offered at $3 and another from the same category at $7 - without much difference in quality - they'll probably go for the cheaper option. However, these expensive or unattractive products can still serve as a decoy if you add a third item from the same category. If this item costs $6, people will more than likely buy it as they see it as a good compromise. They won't have to buy the cheapest product and risk low quality, but they won't feel like they have to splurge either. In reality, they are still buying the more expensive option - but because of the decoy effect, they are distracted from this fact - and will still be willing to go for it. Not only that, but because they are so happy to save on this particular item, they may also decide to add an extra item to their cart.

Using Game Techniques

Game techniques, or gamification of the market, is a relatively new method - which arose with the popularity of video games. While using game mentality in a non-game environment may sound strange, it's actually one of the most impactful persuasion methods. Marketers rely on the same mentality games use during their sessions - persuading potential buyers with game elements. The added motivation enriches the user experience. It's tempting and mentally gripping, enticing the buyers to their products, just as games do with hardcore players. Gamification of user experience allows marketers to let users experience a unique journey and even give them an achievement at the end. It stimulates the drive to reach the end goal, the most intrinsic motivation gamers and non-gamers have. This technique either lets the buyer set the goals they want to achieve at the end of the shopping experience or chooses the target for them. Either way, the company selling the products or services also achieves its goal.

Other Persuasion Techniques

Apart from marketing, persuasion techniques can be used to influence people in several other sectors of life. Below, you'll see a selection of strategies you can apply for a broad range of purposes, regardless of your level of expertise in persuasion.

Appealing to a Reason

The most influential messages are always based on valid reasons. Learning how to use sound logic is another one of the primary persuasion techniques recommended for beginners. Most people respond well to persuasive messages when presented with a valid reason for why your idea is better. Once you understand how to appeal to the critical thinking abilities of others while avoiding falsities and manipulation, you'll be able to persuade them to do small tasks for you.

Appealing to an Emotion

Unfortunately, not all people respond well to a reason, as they don't like to ponder on why things happen. Instead, they rely on emotions like compassion, hope, happiness, fear, and sadness to guide them through life. You'll need more than just a simple application of traditional arguments to persuade them. Devising appropriate messages that appeal to people's emotions and senses is another must for developing highly efficient persuasion skills. You can also combine approaches and raise the odds of persuading those around you even more.

Appealing to the Speaker's Character

Messages offered by a speaker who listeners trust will always be more persuasive. While this is also true for the written word, the spoken word carries even more weight in the eyes of the audience. If the listeners know that the speaker is knowledgeable about the topic, they'll view the speaker's character as more appealing and be more likely to believe anything the speaker says. Therefore, the speaker's persuasion will be more effective. Keep in mind that this only works if the persuader is knowledgeable. Otherwise, the entire plan will fail as soon as someone from the audience examines it critically.

While speakers must indicate to audiences that they are knowledgeable and passionate about the topic from the start, this effort will be more than worth it. When it comes to building character, the delivery of the message is equally important as the content. Apart from indicating their expertise, persuaders must remain confident while conversing with others. When it's time for the persuader to speak, they should be prepared to deliver the message fluidly. Stumbling over your words, using verbal influences, and filler words all destroy credibility and need to be avoided when delivering a speech.

The Confident Approach

While some people are naturally persuasive, others find convincing people to see their point of view more challenging. Working on your confidence will make it easier to steer a conversation in the direction you want. As soon as you start expressing yourself with more confidence, your messages will become more concise and trustworthy. The most persuasive speakers always prepare what they want to say and repeat it in their minds before saying it out loud. This way, they can be more confident in appearing sure of themselves, no matter how tricky the conversation.

The 'Framing' Method

The "framing" method is nothing more than carefully relaying information in a way that determines how listeners interpret your message. The same information can be explained in several ways, so it sounds different even though the exact same thing is being described in both cases. It can sound positive, negative, or somewhere in the middle, depending on the description you choose to use. This is another popular technique used in political campaigns, especially when debating opponents. Politician use framing to get their audience to adopt their point of view using these fundamental elements:

- **The Right Approach**: Carefully constructing the argument around positive facts is far more effective than the use of negative arguments and will help you persuade others.

- **Appropriate Wording:** Choosing your words is equally important if you want to explain your viewpoint. Not only do you have to be fluent, but the more accurately you describe the situation, the more knowledgeable you seem.

- **The Correct Placement:** You'll need to learn the right time and place to talk to the right people about the right topics. You have far better chances of communicating your point if the people you are speaking to are actually interested in what you have to say.

Including Yourself in the Picture

When showcasing the benefits of accepting your point of view, don't just say "you - the people/audience" will enjoy the benefits you're speaking about. Use the word "we" to ensure that your opinion is relevant and inclusive to everyone, including yourself. This gives the appearance that you care about what benefits everyone and not just your own interests. It also makes people around you feel like they belong to a community or a team, which is far more appealing than working alone.

Explaining the Benefits

Explaining the benefits of accepting your point of view is another great way to influence people. This means underlining how the listener specifically can take advantage of your approach to any issue. Just as marketers use incentives to get people to buy products and services, so can you convince people to align with your values. You don't have to offer incentives like big companies, but it doesn't hurt to make it personal. For example, if you promise a favor in return for theirs, make sure the favor you promise will benefit them personally. They'll feel appreciated and will be much more easily persuaded.

Emphasizing Freedom of Choice

Saying to potential customers that they are free to choose between buying or declining a product or service increases the number of sales. By simply giving them the freedom of choice, you can easily persuade your listeners to accept your opinions. People like to think they are choosing to support a cause, which means it's one of the most straightforward strategies you can employ in dark psychology. You simply have to remind them that the decision is theirs, and in most cases, they will soon end up agreeing with you.

The 'It's Working for Others' Approach

In most cases, you can also easily persuade someone by simply saying that accepting your opinion has proven to work for others. As soon as you mention that others have adopted your point, your audience will start thinking that there must be something to it and consider employing the approach themselves. This technique is often used in industries where having a product or service used by many people is an advantage.

Limit Your Availability

Just as marketers restrict the ability of their sales, discounts, and products to create scarcity, so, too, can you limit your availability to inquiries about your opinion. Hint that you have about an interesting piece of information, but don't disclose too much. This will make it seem that the information you have to give is exclusive, piquing people's curiosity. An attractive piece of information like this will always find its way to the interested parties, and people who learn what it is will be more likely to agree with you.

Using Data and Evidence

You should also gather data and other tangible pieces of evidence to support your beliefs. This has become particularly important in recent years when the number of academic studies, articles about good industry practices, and surveys you can find online has seen exponential growth. Presenting any of these will add more weight to your message. If you are introducing a new concept to a certain target group, you can also compile data about the successful application of this concept by other groups.

Creating an Anchor Point

Creating an anchor point in persuasion refers to planting a subtle cognitive bias that'll help you influence the listener's decisions. It will allow you to negotiate better deals - whether you use it at your workplace or when buying big-ticket items at a store. When a person tries to make a decision, they'll always reach an anchoring point. This point is the first opportunity they have to make a decision and will serve as a stepping stone for subsequent decision-making processes. This works particularly efficiently when trying to negotiate numbers so they will be more favorable for you. By suggesting a number first, you're creating an anchor point, which allows the negotiations to go in your favor. And if you can't reach an agreement about the number, the other party will most likely return to the starting point and agree on it.

Using Body Language

Sometimes, using body language will help you persuade people more than any eloquent speech would. Here are some ways you can influence people by using your body language alone:

- **Playing with Your Eyebrows:** Raising your eyebrows occasionally signals a friendly disposition.

- **Smiling Naturally:** Makes you seem approachable, and people will be drawn to you no matter what you have to say.

- **Keeping Your Arms in an Open Position:** This position signals that you feel comfortable around the people you're surrounded by and don't mind being approached by them.

- **Wearing Complementary Colors:** This will help you stand out - in a good way. Being put together well makes you seem more appealing and friendly.

- **Showing Your Palms:** Gesturing with your hands while opening your palms upwards is a great way to add to your story.

- **A Visible Neck:** Leaving your neck uncovered shows that you are unthreatening and easy to approach.

Chapter 3

What Is Mind Control?

After persuasion, the second most commonly used tool in dark psychology is mind control. But what exactly is mind control? This term encompasses all actions taken to change someone's thought patterns, emotions, and resulting actions. In a sense, it's very similar to persuasion, except it takes a bit more effort and time to accomplish. Persuasion is a subtle method, while mind control can be all-consuming, taking over the target's entire life. For example, persuasion will make a person think about buying an item, but they'll spend time considering all their options. With mind control, however, they'll be able to think of nothing else but buying the item as soon as possible. Another difference between the two techniques is that while persuasion is a widely accepted psychological tool, mind control is often viewed as an obscure method with no other intention than to hurt someone.

Mind control isn't simply making people do something because you want it done. It requires critical thinking, calculating the other person's moves, and reacting to them with your own strategy. Slowly but surely, you have to make them believe that it was their idea to do it in the first place. Meanwhile, you must hide your own goal and suppress your natural inclination to react even if things don't go as planned. This means you'll need to know yourself as well.

When and Why Is Mind Control Used?

Just like persuasion, mind control can also be used literally anywhere. Here are some examples of how mind control can be used in different situations.

Establishing an Authority Figure

In politics, religion, and any other sector where one person influences large masses, control is achieved by building up a person to be seen as a highly distinguished authoritarian figure. People are led to believe that this person either has the expertise to provide accurate information or that their interests are secondary to those of the people they represent. Mind control only works if the authority is strong and trustworthy enough. This way, the targets will believe the leader only acts in their best interest.

Encouraging Education

Parents often control their children's minds by offering them rewards for good behavior and grades. They encourage them to continue the positive behavior, promising better future career opportunities and social standing. For a child to believe this, they'll often need to be given the attention and gifts they desire. When they receive their reward, they become even more motivated to continue their exemplary behavior and maintain good grades.

Creating a Feeling of Superiority

Marketers often use people's need to feel superior to control their audience's minds. By making you believe that adopting a new mindset, will make you become someone superior, and the new behavior will elevate you above the rest of your social circle. Unfortunately, nowadays, more and more people feel the need to be unique and better than everyone else - which is why they're so vulnerable to mind control.

Motivating Buyers

Mind control is used to motivate potential buyers to browse through products in a store. It's also used for converting leads for sales in e-commerce. As soon as a visitor clicks on a product or service, the seller starts to monitor their behavior. If needed, they are offered help and incentives like discounts to make them buy the items.

Creating Panic

Creating panic is a widespread form of mind control that plays on people's greatest fears. It's used everywhere, from politics to healthcare or any other situation where an influencer feels the need to instill fear into people. The audience is led to believe that in order to avoid their deepest fears coming true, they must accept the solution offered by the influencer- which is to accept the influencer's beliefs and behavior.

Creating Contempt for the Competition

When two different influencers compete for control of one target group, they will back up the fear and authority factors by throwing in another strategy. They'll do their best to create contempt for the competition, representing them in the worst light. This prevents the audience from listening to the competition and possibly destroys any progress they've made with the target audience.

Pumping up Prices

Popular brands are known for selling products and services that don't reflect their quality. They advertise them as must-haves, something that could improve your life in a way that no other product or service can. Of course, people could buy the same quality for much cheaper - and often from the same brand as well. But because they are made to believe that the big brand's product is better because it costs more, they'll purchase it anyway.

Avoiding Responsibility

People often use mind control to avoid personal responsibility in legal or financial matters. A perfect example of this would be someone getting a parking ticket and arguing their way out of it by convincing the authorities that they had the right to park where they did.

How Is Mind Control Achieved?

Mind control takes a complex strategy and several steps to complete. Here is a simplified version of how it works.

Doing All the Thinking

The first rule of mind control is never to ask someone to think about your ideas. Between all their daily obligations, they'll probably have no time or inclination to do this anyway. You have to do all the thinking for them and hit them with a conclusion they'll have no choice but to accept.

Launching Thoughts in Motion

Launching mind control into action often takes a bold move. Offering a powerful idea can make people question their previous beliefs. After this, all you need to do is step back and see how their minds are being changed.

Starting Out Small

People who've mastered the art of mind control never ask for too much upfront. When trying to change someone's mind, it's always better to ask for a small compromise to start with. When you reach it, you can take advantage of the trust you've gained and begin taking more and more.

Representing Something Greater

Another crucial factor in changing someone's mind is representing something greater than yourself. People trust leaders, authority figures, and even social media influencers because they believe they are acting for unselfish reasons. Making people empathize with your cause is a great way to get and keep their attention on your point of view.

Being Bold

The most successful mind control strategies work because people aren't afraid to use them. While advertisements, media, and other public campaigns are often judged for being shameless, their efforts always pay off. Being bold and standing up for what you believe is a crucial element that ties together all the previous ones. When you believe in something, you don't ask people to accept it. You promote it, and demand people acknowledge it as the truth.

Skills You Need to Become Better at Mind Control

Learning to control people's minds takes an open and highly active mindset. By working on the following skills, you can evolve into this state and be able to change people's minds about anything and anytime you want to.

Sociability

If you're serious about learning mind control, you must be assertive in your communication with everyone around you. Socialize, network, and take every opportunity you can get to study how people's minds work. Whether you engage in deep conversation or chat about the weather, it doesn't matter. What matters is that you observe how people react to your words and behavior.

Studiousness

Mind control is a skill developed over time. Learning how to use it efficiently will require you to continue constantly researching the subject. How it works and what aspects of the target's life it affects can change over time and may differ in the various situations you'll encounter in life. Be curious, and feel free to look up and test various strategies.

Strategic Thinking

To change someone's mind, you'll need to use a tactic that overpowers their own beliefs. This tactic may need to be modified as you explore your target's thought patterns. Continuously working on and tweaking your strategy when necessary will allow you to control every factor that could influence your outcome. An efficient strategy is one that the target believes has too many benefits to turn down or disregard.

Listening Abilities

Learning how to balance eagerness and your listening abilities is crucial for achieving efficient mind control. Sometimes you just have to step back, listen and contemplate what you hear. Your audience will appreciate being heard, and you'll learn a lot about them. This will also give you time to come up with what to say to your audience to change their minds.

The Effects of Mind Control

The effects of mind control are far-reaching and often depend on the cognitive capacity of both the controller and the person being influenced. Here is a list of common effects mind control can have on the recipient.

Being Kept in the Dark

When someone's mind is being changed, they are rarely aware of what's happening to them. The recipient's thoughts are being modified slowly until they finally align with the point of view of the person controlling them. For example, the situation when you don't have any intention of trying a product but are presented with convincing testimonials through ads, and suddenly you are buying the product. You can also apply the same principle to asking for a favor from a friend. Send subtle messages until the friend ends up doing your bidding, thinking it was their own idea to do so. In most cases, it's about fulfilling the controller's inner needs and giving them power. But it can also be about influencing someone to try something that may be beneficial for them.

Living in a Controlled Environment

People succumb to mind control because contrary to popular belief, it's not only their thoughts and minds that are being controlled. The social and sometimes even physical environment is also under the controller's watchful eye. By attaching specific rules to the idea, you want them to adopt and back this up with a structured plan and assignments; you can control how a person behaves and who they interact with. Working on these small tasks will keep them busy and focused on digesting the idea or attitude until they accept it.

A Sense of Powerlessness Appears

Whether the target realizes they are being controlled or not, they may have a sense of powerlessness. Since people tend to surround themselves with like-minded individuals, this means that most of the time, the target has a social circle with the same ideas, beliefs, and attitudes as theirs. To gain control over them, the influencer alienates everyone whose beliefs don't align with theirs. This loss of social support system causes powerlessness, which lasts until they realize that there are also people whose ideas align with their new ones. In the worst-case scenario, this is used to make the target lose all personal power, eradicating their self-confidence and intuition. However, when used for positive purposes, mind control only has to change what people's intuition is telling them. They only have to modify their understanding of reality - not completely erase it. This way, if members of the target social circle counteract their new viewpoint, they'll be able to defend it with valid arguments.

The Reward-And-Punishment Loop

Along with the tasks that keep them busy, influencers often place rewards and punishments in the target's path. Targets always get positive feedback on supporting the beliefs of the person controlling their mind. Whereas when their own ideas and attitudes surface, they get punished by being left out of something important. However, the person doing the controlling must be careful to keep up the balance of reward and punishment. People can't be rewarded or punished all the time, but they can be kept in a loop that lets them repeat both behaviors. While this sounds somewhat counterproductive in terms of changing someone's mind, slow changes are more likely to stick than quick ones. Or in other words, punishments play just as much of a role in adapting to new behaviors as rewards do.

Need for Approval

As the target earns their rewards and finishes their tasks while trying to avoid punishment, they are constantly looking for the controller's approval. Because they understand the benefits of accepting the other person's point of view, the target will willingly exhibit behavior that is likely to get them the validation they need. They'll try to avoid any chance of disapproval or rejection. They also won't question any new beliefs and behaviors because it doesn't feel right for them to do so.

A Closed System

Efficient mind control techniques create a closed system that relies on the controller's creation. This system doesn't leave much room for compromise or feedback on how the target feels about the changes happening to them. Targets often think that their input in their own lives isn't validated by the person controlling them. They may also feel that the person they are trying to emulate has nothing to lose - while they may face several losses while their relationship persists.

The Benefits of Mind Control

Despite common misconceptions, mind control is an inherently good practice. In fact, it carries several benefits, including the ones described below. Some are more advantageous for the person afflicted by the control than others.

Gives You Power

The power of mind control has been a much-debated subject. From religion to politics to social media, elements of mind control can be found everywhere. While the power of mass control by the media or society doesn't always positively impact the subject's life, the individual effects of mind control can. There is nothing more empowering than having the mental strength to control not only your own mind but the minds of others as well. Knowing you can positively impact someone else's life can be incredibly liberating. It allows you to focus your mind, not letting yourself lose sight of your goals. Once you set your intention to influence someone else's mind and you start seeing the positive results, you'll be inspired to continue on this path.

Helps Avoid Conflicts

Your thoughts, emotions and behaviors are all interconnected and interact with each other daily. The more dominant someone's thoughts are, the more emotions they spike, leading to assertive, agitated, and sometimes impulsive behavior. When you encounter someone whose thoughts are just as dominant as yours, you are more likely to be in conflict with them. However, if you can learn how to control their minds, making their thoughts less dominant, the less they'll feel the need to react emotionally. This keeps your emotions down too, and conflict can be avoided because you'll have nothing to fight about. You'll be able to see things from a different perspective, allowing you to change tactics if you need to. This will enable you to develop more productive mind control strategies with the same person, if necessary, and everyone else in the future. Once again, this is a benefit that all media channels and platforms have become aware of and use. If one form of control proves to be counteractive, making the audience react negatively, they simply switch to another one.

Health Benefit

Mind control is also often used by therapists working with patients suffering from psychological trauma. The distraction and control it provides come with numerous health benefits. It allows the person to reduce the number of sleepless nights caused by anxiety, depression, night terrors, and disruptive sleep patterns. While mind control doesn't eliminate them completely, it alleviates other symptoms of mental health conditions, giving the person being influenced a sense of inner peace. They'll soon start to realize that there is a light at the end of the tunnel, and it's more than worth fighting for their goal, which is getting healthy. Mind control may take a person's mind off of physical symptoms too. It has been successfully used for pain management in several chronic conditions.

Facilitates Communication

Recurring thoughts, emotions, and behaviors become ingrained as memories in your subconscious. Later, when your mind identifies clues related to these memories, it uses them to repeat the actions automatically. Over time, these repetitions become part of your everyday life. One of the ways you use them is in communication. The more you try to control someone's mind, the more of these little clues you plant in their subconscious until they unconsciously adopt them as if they were products of their own mind. After a while, when conversing with someone, you won't have to repeat the entire set of information anymore. Only repeating a few keywords will trigger the thoughts, emotions, and behavior you want them to express. It becomes a part of them just as much as it's a part of you. They will stop shrugging it off as they did in the beginning, facilitating communication between you.

Provides Positive Distraction

Changing someone's ideas and attitude often opens their minds about certain beliefs, so they learn to accept other points of view. While they work on adopting the new thought patterns, their minds enjoy a respite from the multitude of stimuli they receive and the stress of daily life. This benefit is also tied to ingrained memories as the mind often brings up the new beliefs as positive distractions, which helps consolidate them even more in one's subconscious.

Brings Relief to the Recipient

Not having to worry about certain things can bring enormous relief for a person affected by mind control. As mentioned before, the basic philosophy of mind control dictates that you should do the thinking instead of the person you are trying to influence. Consequently, they'll be happy to abide by your influence and rules if it means they don't have to figure out whether it's right or wrong to do so. While this may sound counterproductive and complicated, it actually isn't. Just think about all the obvious solutions that advertisements offer to everyday problems. Most of us are ready to accept them because we are relieved that we don't have to find a solution ourselves.

Chapter 4

Methods of Mind Control

The number of approaches to mind control varies depending on several factors. The definition of the technique, the type of psychological tools used, and even the cognitive functions of the person being influenced can affect which methods are used. This chapter discusses the most common mind control methods used in different areas of life. It explains what each strategy consists of, how it's done, and when it's used.

Brainwashing

The terms "mind control" and "brainwashing" are often used interchangeably. When, in fact, brainwashing is only one form of mind control - and the most difficult one at that. Brainwashing means reforming someone's thoughts through some form of social influence. Many people know how emulating others in their environment can change their thoughts and behavior. Because of this, they are conditioned to believe that brainwashing also happens frequently.

However, to do it successfully, you'll need to combine three different approaches: persuasion, compliance, and education. The education part suggests to the target that they must do something or express their beliefs in a certain way because it's the right thing to do. Persuasion, as you know, relies on positive reinforcement. The compliance method only aims to make a change based on the brainwasher's goals. The combination of all three factors makes for a severe and invasive form of mind control technique.

Brainwashing changes someone's attitudes without their consent, which can only be applied in specific conditions, such as wartime, prison, or cult settings. In these cases, the target is isolated, often hurt, and dependent on the brainwasher for food, shelter, and other basic human necessities. This gives the brainwasher complete control over the target's mind and allows them to convince the target to believe in anything they want them to. The brainwasher slowly chips away the target's natural defenses, reading their identity. After this, they can replace it with a new identity consisting of beliefs and behaviors that allow them to maintain control.

Since creating confusion and self-doubt are critical elements of brainwashing, without them, the method cannot be used. Only when these are present, combined with a sense of guilt and a narrow mindset, can people be trapped into being brainwashed. All these elements must be present in extreme forms, which rarely happens - making brainwashing a rare occurrence.

Hypnosis

Hypnosis is a method that relies on creating a heightened state of awareness, in which one's focus is shifted towards ideas and attitudes suggested by the person doing the hypnosis. Some compared this state to being asleep because that is what it feels like. During sleep, the mind is relaxed enough to work through different stimuli it receives during waking hours. However, unlike being asleep, one is conscious during hypnosis. They can hear everything suggested by the hypnotist - only their minds can accept the suggestions faster because it's not overwhelmed by other conscious thoughts. If the target's mind is already relaxed, the first step (calming) may not even be necessary.

Hypnosis is an approach that relies on the following core principles:

- **Mutual Benefits:** You may suggest you need their help just as much as they require yours.

- **Enhanced Recognition:** Making the subject repeat the suggestion out loud allows their mind to accept it.

- **Sensory Stimulation:** Thinking about the suggestion often stimulates one or more of the subject's senses.

- **Physical Stimulation:** Thinking about the suggestion changes how the body behaves.

- **Feedback:** You'll also need to verify that the suggestion is accepted by asking the subject about their thoughts on it.

- **Making Use of Acceptance:** As soon as the suggestion is accepted, you can start working on changing the attitude and the subject's behavior.

- **Being Confident:** Your attitude is the key to success - the more confident you are in your skills, the more likely you'll hypnotize someone.

Commonly used techniques of hypnotism include:

- **Support:** Affirm the target of your seemingly unconditional support.

- **Ambiguity:** Taking advantage of a focused state to implant several ideas.

- **Confirmation**: Affirming the person that they are getting what they want.

- **Capturing the Attention:** The target's mind is occupied by the suggestion.

- **Testing Suggestibility**: handclasps and similar methods are often used to test the target's readiness to accept the suggestion.

- **Arm Relaxation:** The target suggests that they'll feel like their arms are floating.

- **Linking Body Parts:** As the target's arms relax, the feeling spreads to the rest of their body.

- **Confirmation of Notice:** The target is asked whether they've noticed their relaxed state.

- **Pause:** The target is given time to assimilate to their new state.

- **Repeat:** Saying relax to the target further relaxes them.

- **Tensing Muscles:** The target is asked to tense their muscles in order to relax their body.

- **Vague Suggestions:** People react better to vague ideas than to specific ones that stand against their values.

- **Visualization:** Asking the target to imagine a crucial aspect of the idea presented to them allows their mind to assimilate it faster.

A key element of hypnosis is to ensure the targets allow the suggestions to penetrate their minds. To be hypnotized, a person doesn't have to be gullible, hurt, or weak-minded. Nothing the hypnotizer can suggest can be accepted unless the target wants to acknowledge it. Being hypnotized won't allow the other person to take complete control. The subject is always in control and will not do anything that doesn't fit with their core principles. If a notion goes against your core values, you probably won't let your mind focus on it. And neither will anyone else. Even if you've suggested something like that to another person during hypnosis, they will likely just snap out of that relaxed state you've put them into. That means suggestions need to be presented in a way that is appealing to the target. For example, suggesting to someone that they behave in a way that likely leads to injuries is not going to work because the idea of getting hurt is unacceptable. On the other hand, if you suggest accepting an attitude that leads to material gain or other benefits, they'll be willing to focus on the idea.

Another critical element to note is that the target does not always remember the suggestions - at least not consciously. Hypnosis is done to almost everyone on a daily basis - but many of us aren't even aware that we were hypnotized. For example, creating compelling commercials or movie scenes can make the audience so engrossed in watching it that they don't even notice what's happening around them. The media often appeals to people's emotions to sell their suggestions by heightening the feelings to the point that they change people's behavior. They make people so focused on the specific scenes that their minds and bodies start to react even without them being aware of doing anything. Their ultimate goal is to create empathy toward what is happening on the screen.

Repetition

Forced repetition of the same idea is another commonly used mind control method. It's a simple strategy, which is why it's often recommended for people just dipping their toes into the realm of dark psychology. The first step is to formulate a simple but compelling message and plant it in someone's mind. After that, you'll keep repeating it to them as long as necessary to make it sink in. The easier it is for them to understand, the less you'll have to work on repeating it.

Repetition is a technique that relies on social proof. People look for the approval of their thoughts, beliefs, attitudes, and behaviors from others in their social circle. To make the repetition approach work, you must suggest an idea they can verify by noticing it in those around them. If they see that everyone else accepts the message, they will be willing to acknowledge it. Seeing that social proof acts as a form of repetition itself.

This approach has been used by the media and authorities for many years. However, recently, another form of repetition has emerged. Positive affirmations used for building self-confidence and growth are the newest example of repetition at work. People use positive affirmation to convince themselves (or others) that thinking and behaving in a specific way is beneficial for them. They do this by repeating the same positive message day after day until they start believing it.

Repetition is particularly effective in group settings where everyone is looking for validation from each other. They're afraid of being shamed if they speak out or act without first being validated. They wait until they can be sure they won't be in disagreement with anyone else in the group. This is because whoever is planting these social proofs is making suggestions by asking questions the members can't answer without changing their beliefs. They make the members believe that the only way to answer these questions truthfully is to agree with the leader's idea. While they may notice that they haven't received an immediate answer to the questions, repeating the same message makes the members think they can reveal the answers themselves.

Conversion Techniques

As its name implies, conversion is a mind control approach that relies on converting one's values, beliefs, and attitudes into different ones. It's a simple method that involves developing a different way of thinking- and because of this, it can be applied in a broad range of situations. Some of the most common techniques used to convert someone's beliefs into different ideas are:

- **Establishing Authority:** The target is made to believe in an absolute authority figure that they have no way to challenge.

- **Breaking Habits:** Putting people under pressure until they start believing that changing their ideas is the only way to get relief.

- **Changing Core Values:** The target's core values are challenged to the point where they start to question what's right and what's wrong.

- **Providing the Opportunity to Confess:** By acknowledging undesirable past actions, targets are willing to move on toward new beliefs.

- **Dietary Changes:** Suggest the target to consume food that weakens their cognitive resolve.

- **Opening the Mind:** Getting the target to become open to new ideas limits their ability to rationalize old beliefs.

- **Engaging Behavior:** The target is engaged in a conversation or other behavior that allows you to draw them in.

- **Physical and Mental Exhaustion:** If the target is exhausted, they'll be less likely to resist the conversion.

- **Drawing out Guilt:** This method refers to thoughts and behaviors the target is unsatisfied about.

- **Presenting a Higher Purpose:** By associating the desired attitude with an unselfish and noble cause, the target can be convinced of its benefits.

- **Destruction of Identity:** By chipping away at the target person, you're creating space for a new identity.

- **Illogical Thinking:** Pointing out that the target's attitude may seem irrational in other people's eyes makes them reevaluate their beliefs.

- **Thought Control**: Any thoughts the target may have to dismiss your arguments are blocked by other, more powerful messages.

- **Gradual Conversion:** Making slow progress by gradually changing the person's beliefs and increasing the difficulty of the demands.

- **Banking on Isolation**: The target is separated from others who may send them dissuading messages.

- **Emotional Hooks:** Lonely people are more vulnerable to conversion, especially to the suggestion that by accepting an idea, they'll have access to emotional attachments.

- **Persistent Demands:** Sending persuasive messages to the target until their defenses crumble.

- **Radicalization:** Changing one's ideas into more radical ones.

- **Using Specific Language:** People's thoughts can be easily converted by using a language that exudes power and offers a new meaning to existing beliefs.

Conversion is often used in religion, politics, larger social groups, and other organizations influenced by specific ideologies.

Propaganda

Propaganda is a tool that leads to control over people's thoughts and beliefs, affecting their reactions. It finds and collects all the ideas people in a targeted group will accept as universal truth. Employing messages that people won't question, propaganda can make people align with any ideology they represent. This ideology can represent any religious, philosophical, or political belief people already believe in. It's only a question of enhancing their thoughts about it through consistent and affirmative messages. Many ideologies use propaganda to promote what they stand for. It gives them power over their target audience. They also deem any other ideas or counterpoints invalid and sometimes even harmful for the people's safety and security.

There is a unique quality to propaganda that distinguishes it from other, more obvious mind control methods. Successful propaganda is always hidden behind meaningful and supposed reasonable messages, so the people under its influence aren't even aware of what's happening to them. They simply accept the truth the communicator is offering without question or noticing the hidden motive behind it. The communicator will appear to be someone trying to help people and not control their minds. Even if the target realizes that they are being manipulated and expresses defiance, the person in charge often has other methods to keep them at bay. Due to its covert nature, it's easy to see why propaganda is successfully used on large groups of people.

In order to be effective, propaganda relies on several specific conditions. One of these is control over mass communication channels. If the person in charge has power over these channels, they can ensure only the "right" messages are being promoted. The list of people who may hold authority over the information certain groups can access includes company owners, teachers, parents, influencers, politicians, and other authoritative figures. Whoever this authority figure is, they always need to make people align with their ideas or perceive reality in a different way.

Power

Power is often tied to one or more of the other mind control techniques. Its definition is what the person exerts it wants or desires from other people. The fulfillment of desires often depends on whether other people behave, think, or feel in a certain way. Using your power to influence others can help you take control over people's minds, changing every or any of these three aspects of human attitude. In fact, this core principle can be applied to all other methods used in dark psychology. From authority figures to social media to advertising agencies - everyone relies on their own ability to establish and showcase their power.

To use your power, you must first understand it. More importantly, you'll need to understand other people's power. You need to use your skills carefully - just in case you run into someone more powerful than you. You should also avoid the excessive display of power at all costs. This leads to people becoming agitated, which may trigger their own need to exert their power. Instead, you should use your skills in a subtle way - so they don't even notice you're doing it.

Power can also be used indirectly - and very effectively so. For example, you can plant an idea in someone's mind about the benefits of using their powers. If they comply, they are actually gaining power on your behalf without you putting too much effort into it. Threats are also commonly used as displays of power and are often combined with other methods. Whether they're physical or psychological, threats can be an incredibly effective tool for mind control. As long as the target believes you hold power over them, you'll always have a way of changing their minds.

Persuading with Willpower

The use of willpower is a crucial tool of mind control. While simple persuasion only gives people a nudge to start thinking and acting differently, persuading with willpower entails far more. A person's willpower determines the course of their actions, reactions, thoughts, and emotions. To change any or all of this, you must exert a significant amount of willpower of your own. This means engaging in a battle of wills with the goal of becoming the victor and finally persuading others to align with your beliefs or attitude.

Here are a few ways people can be persuaded through their willpower.

- **Build-Up:** Slowly chip away at someone's willpower until it weakens enough for you to overpower them. After this, it'll be much easier to persuade them to do your bidding or align with your beliefs.

- **Slow Drips:** Like when a tap is dripping water. You're sending small but repetitive and compelling messages until they comply with your wishes. The messages have to be friendly and positive.

- **The Escalation Method:** Continuing to send messages that slowly reveal your willpower often escalates into victory. It starts by politely explaining your point; then, you find a way to prove it before using this as leverage against the other person's will.

- **Involving Others:** Involving other people to support your case can be a powerful way to show a person that you can go against their willpower. Just make sure the people you've involved will support your beliefs and attitudes unconditionally.

- **Offering Support**: Seeking moral support from people close to you can enhance your willpower, allowing you to overpower your competition. Even if your supporters won't get involved, knowing they stand beside you will boost your confidence.

- **Being Persistent:** Persuading with willpower is about who can stay in the game longer. By showing that you're willing to remain persistent, you are signaling that you won't stop until you've reached your goal.

- **Using Eye Contact:** Intently gazing into someone's eye during a period can be incredibly intimidating. It shows that you don't even need words to show how superior your willpower is.

- **Using Specific Language:** Using loaded words can help you impose your will on others. Words that sound meaningful, assertive, and emphasize a strong point are particularly effective.

- **The Personal Attack Method:** Attacking someone's personal beliefs can be another great way to make them question their attitude. Sometimes all it takes is pointing out a mistake they've made as a result of their beliefs, and you'll be able to overpower them.

Chapter 5

What Is Gaslighting?

The term "gaslighting" has been gaining huge popularity in the last few years, as more and more people have been using it to describe a certain toxic behavior that often occurs within relationships. You might think that "gaslighting" is a new or modern term. However, it has been around for almost a century. The origin of the word goes back to 1938 British playwright Patrick Hamilton's play "Gas Light" was first released. In 1944, the play was adapted into a popular movie called "Gaslight." It led more people to learn about this toxic behavior and begin associating it with the movie title, Gaslight.

The movie is about a husband who manipulates his wife to make her question her sense of reality and persuade her that she is losing her mind. He wants to drive her insane, so he can commit her to a mental institution and take her money. The movie was named "Gaslight" because, in one scene, the husband turns gaslights on in the attic, causing them to flicker in the house. When the wife notices the flickering and asks him about it, he tells her that she sees things. This is meant to insert self-doubt into her mind and make her question her perceptions. This is how the term "gaslighting" came to be.

Gaslighting is a form of manipulation and psychological and emotional abuse. Just like the husband in the movie, a gaslighter is someone who manipulates a person or a group of people to make them question their perception, reality, and memory. This behavior is extremely dangerous to the victim's mental health as they stop believing in their own reality and accept the manipulator's recollection of events instead. In other words, the gaslighter presents their victim with a false narrative to mislead them and make them question themselves and their own judgments. Eventually, they lose their self-esteem, confidence, and mental stability.

Gaslighting doesn't happen right away, as the manipulator usually starts with small and insignificant incidents and then builds up to bigger and more serious ones so they can eventually exert complete control and power over their victims. The victims then find themselves unable to lead normal day-to-day lives where they can make their own decisions, think clearly, or have a clear sense of their own well-being as they become completely dependent on the abuser.

Although gaslighting is mainly associated with romantic relationships, it can also occur in all other relationships. A friend, family member, co-worker, or boss can use gaslighting tactics to control you. In most cases, gaslighters aren't mentally stable individuals and may suffer from one or more mental disorders. Presently, gaslighting itself isn't recognized as a mental disorder. However, this doesn't make it any less dangerous or harmful to the victim's mental health.

When and Why People Use Gaslighting

Gaslighting usually occurs when there is an uneven power dynamic. The manipulator is usually someone in power or, at least, more powerful than their victims. For instance, the term "gaslighting" was used by many people to describe Donald Trump's behavior during his presidential campaign and time in office. He would say something that the whole world heard and understood, then later deny it and say that he had never said that, nor would he ever think of saying something like that. Even though there was proof that contradicted him and showed that he had, in fact, said those words, he used gaslighting and his position of power to manipulate the public. He created his own reality and manipulated people to believe that he was the only true reality. Judging by how many supporters Donald Trump still has, it is clear that his tactics worked.

When the manipulator uses their power to gaslight others, this can scare the victims from ever speaking up, standing up for themselves, or taking action to change the power dynamic in their favor. Victims in romantic relationships are often afraid of challenging their manipulator. They believe that their partner will leave them if they ever speak up, so they stay quiet and accept the abuse to please them. The victim is willing to change their own judgments, perceptions, and reality just to avoid conflict with the manipulator. Usually, when the gaslighter is someone close to you, like your spouse or parent, you will find it hard to believe or even accept that this person is gaslighting you. You end up accepting their reality because you refuse to believe that someone you love and trust will end up manipulating you. The gaslighter knows this and takes advantage of your trust to control you.

Gaslighting is more common in romantic relationships. Again, the power dynamic is at play here, where the more powerful person manipulates the other. According to various research, gaslighting usually occurs in heterosexual relationships where a man exerts his control over a woman. In fact, gaslighting is often associated with domestic violence, as many domestic violence victims have reported experiencing gaslighting along with other forms of abuse. Male manipulators take advantage of the old and sexist stereotype that women are overly emotional and irrational while men are more reasonable. They use it to weaken their victims by making them believe their narrative since they know better; they are the more reasonable sex, after all. Although the feminist movement is now stronger than ever, and women have been advocating to move away from these stereotypes, they still persist to this day with some men.

Your doctor can also employ gaslighting behavior thanks to power dynamics. This also occurs when the doctor is male, and the victim is female. They use the stereotypes associated with women to dismiss their health concerns or to convince them that their symptoms are only in their heads and there is nothing to worry about. Gaslighting is also pretty common in the media, and there is even a name for it "media gaslighting." The media uses this manipulative tactic to brainwash the public or spread propaganda. They are basically telling people how to think so they can fit in, even if this pattern of thought isn't right or healthy. You can see media gaslighting through fake news or false information, which many people witnessed during the Trump and Clinton election campaigns. They may also create a false narrative and a different reality so they can control public opinion. These media outlets don't concern themselves with truth and facts, and they don't even acknowledge them.

Scientists and doctors have also struggled to do their jobs, with the media going around brainwashing people and spreading false information. This was obvious during the COVID- 19 pandemic and the vaccines, with doctors and scientists telling people how vital it is to get vaccinated, while some media outlets kept telling people that COVID-19 is a hoax and the vaccine is a ploy by the government to spy on people. Even though people were dying every day from COVID-19, some people refused to see the truth and facts and bought into the reality created by media gaslighting. The movie "Don't Look Up" perfectly showcases media and political manipulation during a crisis. The movie is about a meteor that is about to hit Earth in a matter of days. However, the media and politicians keep spreading false information and telling people not to panic. Even though scientists appeared on TV screaming, "we are all going to die," the people believed the media and mocked the scientists. Interestingly, all they needed to do was to look up, and they would be able to see the meteor coming towards Earth. This is how gaslighting works. Even when the truth is right in front of you, you won't be able to see it because you have chosen the manipulator's reality and have stopped relying on your own perceptions and judgment.

It can also happen in the workplace. Your boss can use their position of power to make you question your abilities and skills, or a co-worker can spread gossip about you behind your back. This can lead you to question yourself, lose confidence, hate your job, and even ruin your career. For instance, if your boss only gives you negative feedback and never tells you anything positive or gives you constructive criticism, you will begin to believe that you aren't good enough. Or your co-worker spreads gossip about you or makes belittling comments, but when you confront them, they accuse you of being too sensitive or tell you that you don't remember things correctly. The intention here is to make you question your own perceptions and reality and lower your self-esteem.

Some marketing campaigns also rely heavily on gaslighting to manipulate people into buying their products. If you watched the series, Mad Men, then you probably have an idea of what goes on behind the scenes at advertising agencies. Marketing agencies use gaslighting to intentionally mislead people. In fact, advertising is one of the worst forms of gaslighting. Watch an ad on TV, and you will see how brands lie and manipulate people so they can persuade them to buy their products. For instance, many hair care ads promise long, soft, and thick hair when you use their products, or skincare brands promise you perfect skin once you use their products. These are all false promises that exaggerate the effectiveness of a product to increase sales.

Gaslighters are everywhere around you. They can be the people closest to you, the politicians you trust, your boss, who you respect, or the media that you rely on for information. One question remains, why do people use gaslighting? The answer is simple, to exert control. Gaslighters aim to break their victims' spirits and weaken their resistance, confuse them and create chaos in their lives. Meanwhile, the manipulator acts innocent and blameless. This pattern of behavior will make the victim question everything and everyone, including themselves. Once the victim loses faith in themselves, the people in their lives, and even their own reality, their self-esteem suffers, and they lose their own identity.

Some gaslighters are aware of their behavior. Similar to the husband in the original play, they have a plan and execute it to exert control over their victims. One of the most famous gaslighters in the world is serial killer Charles Manson. He was inspired by the book "How to Win Friends and Influence People" by Dale Carnegie. There was a specific line in the book that Manson drew inspiration from, "Let the other fellow feel that the idea is his." Although this is a book that is meant to help people, a psychopath like Manson used it to create a cult that he brainwashed, resulting in the murder of seven people.

Some manipulators learned gaslighting tactics from their parents. For example, a parent who is an addict will abuse their child or suffers from a mental health issue and may gaslight their child to keep quiet about their struggles. Divorced parents also use gaslighting to alienate their children from the other parent. One parent wants to be seen as the hero, so they portray the other parent as the villain. Some parents also blame their children for everything, while other parents still treat their children as perfect beings who don't make mistakes. This kind of upbringing teaches a child to think in absolutes. Simply put, things are either black or white, good or bad. There is no gray or middle ground. They begin acting this way toward others as if something is all bad or all good, which is an unrealistic thought pattern that can create a distorted reality for their victims.

However, not all the children of gaslighters grow up to become gaslighters themselves. In fact, many learn from their parent's mistakes and see this behavior as something to avoid rather than emulate. Some personality disorders can also contribute to a person's ability to gaslight. For instance, someone with an antisocial personality disorder or a narcissistic personality disorder has the need to control those around them. These are people who want to feel important and that others need them, so they exert control to make people around them dependent on them. Narcissists also portray a false image of themselves and often see others from a distorted point of view. They manipulate and gaslight the people in their lives to keep their false image intact and never acknowledge their flaws or admit their mistakes while projecting their own faults onto others.

On the other hand, some gaslighters aren't consciously aware of their behavior. They want their victims to depend only on them. If no one calls them out on their behavior, they will continue their vicious cycle and damage the people around them. For instance, a president who gaslights the public can become a dictator over his own people if no one holds them accountable for their actions. As a result, people will be afraid to speak up, and the gaslighter president will keep exerting power and control.

How Gaslighting Works

Gaslighting is a long and gradual process where the manipulator breaks down a person's perception of their reality and their trust in themselves. As a result, the victim becomes completely dependent on the abuser. It doesn't happen right away, especially in romantic relationships. It starts with one partner gaining their victim's trust by creating what is referred to as the honeymoon period. In this phase, the manipulator only presents their best selves without showing any abusive behavior. Once they gain a person's trust, they start employing their gaslighting tactics, so the victim feels unreliable, thus relying only on their abuser. The victim will depend on their manipulator for everything, losing their identity in the process and giving full control to their abusers. They will never question the manipulator because they have stopped trusting in their abilities and believe that their abuser is always right. In time, this gives the gaslighter power over their victim and makes them unable to leave.

Whenever you are around a gaslighter, you will feel dazed and confused and will question and second guess yourself. You will believe that something is your fault when it isn't or that you are just being too sensitive.

How Gaslighting affects Those Being Persuaded

Gaslighters use this skill to persuade someone to stay in a toxic relationship. When people lose their identity, stop believing in themselves, and question their own reality, what do they have left? This can make a person depressed, insecure, doubtful of themselves, traumatized, lose their self-esteem, and suffer from PTSD symptoms and constant anxiety.

The victim loses faith in their abilities and relinquishes control to their manipulator, allowing them to make all their decisions for them. When their reality is questioned, the victim begins to believe that something is wrong with them and begins questioning their sanity. As they start losing their self-confidence, victims often feel that they are disappointing everyone in their lives. They believe they aren't doing anything right and keep apologizing for who they are and everything they do. Since the gaslighter keeps their victim questioning their memory, the victim begins to wonder if they remember certain events correctly. They stop relying on their memory or their own recollection of events out of fear that they won't accurately remember things.

The victim stops expressing their emotions or standing up for themselves because everything they say is disparaged, including their perception, judgment, and reality. You feel confused and powerless while giving the manipulator a huge influence over your life. This makes the victim easy to manipulate and persuade. When a person loses their identity, they are vulnerable and susceptible to other people's suggestions. They have nothing to rely on as their identity and reality are jeopardized. As a result, whatever the manipulator tells them, they will most likely believe. This was obvious during many elections throughout history by how politicians manipulated and brainwashed the public so they could eventually persuade them to vote for them. Gaslighting is basically a form of persuasion but a dark and negative method that can make victims believe whatever the manipulator is saying, no matter how insane it sounds.

Benefits and Positive Uses of Gaslighting

There is a positive side to everything, and even gaslighting can have its own benefits. Just as lying can be acceptable to make someone feel good about themselves or spare someone's feelings on some occasions, you can use gaslighting to do the same. Although gaslighting is a form of manipulation, you can use it to help others. There are people who don't believe in themselves and their abilities. They don't want to try anything new because they believe they won't succeed in anything. You can use gaslighting as a method of persuasion to change this false reality. Make them believe in themselves and motivate them to take chances and try new things.

Gaslighting can change someone's reality for the better. Instead of letting someone else control that person, you can use gaslighting to empower someone and make them the ones in control of their reality. Some people often live in a distorted and false reality as a result of their low self-esteem or bad upbringing. You can help them move away from this negativity by presenting them with their abilities and positive traits using gaslighting tactics.

You will encounter gaslighters in all sorts of different areas of your life. Your boss, co-workers, parents, best friends, siblings, or spouse may try to gaslight you. The media, advertisements, and politicians also use gaslighting to brainwash the masses and get what they want from them. Using power dynamics, these people exert their control over their victims. There are various types of emotional manipulation out there. It is essential that you differentiate gaslighting from other toxic behaviors. One main thing that sets this behavior apart is the intent to confuse. Gaslighters' main purpose is to confuse their victims so they can weaken them and make them easy to control and manipulate.

However, you can protect yourself from gaslighting and other manipulative tactics. Understanding gaslighting and when and why people do it is the first step to helping you learn about this negative behavior. In the next chapter, you will learn about the tactics gaslighters use so you can spot gaslighting early on before you lose your power and control to someone else.

Chapter 6

Traits of Gaslighters

Certain traits can help you identify gaslighting behavior because although you might think it's an easy behavior to spot, it is anything but that. These people are great manipulators, and you may not be aware of their intentions until it is too late. Some people could even spend their whole lives as victims of gaslighting and under their abuser's control without realizing that something is wrong. As mentioned, a gaslighter can be someone close to you who you never thought would do anything to hurt you. They also don't seem like bad people at first. A gaslighter usually acts like someone who genuinely cares about you and is concerned for your well-being. On the outside, it seems like they only have your best interest at heart, but the truth is way darker and uglier. The only person a gaslighter cares about is themselves. They don't care about you; they only care about what they can get from you after exerting their control over you.

A gaslighter can be friendly and charming when you first meet them, but this is only an act. Eventually, the mask falls off, and their true colors show. If the gaslighter is a narcissist, you can guarantee that their true personality will come out sooner rather than later. Their need to control will take over, and they slowly begin abusing their victims using various methods with only one goal: controlling them. Don't allow yourself to fall into the trap of a gaslighter. Learn to recognize the red flags so you know when you encounter one or help a loved one who may be a victim of gaslighting.

Constant Lying

Lying is a gaslighter's main weapon. This makes sense since gaslighting essentially creates a false narrative to distort the victim's reality. Gaslighters lie with extreme ease; it is a habit and second nature to them. In fact, gaslighters often have twisted personalities and are known to be pathological liars. Catching a gaslighter in a lie isn't easy because these people are pros. However, if you call them out or happen to find proof of their lies and confront them, they will defend themselves with even bigger and stronger lies. They will never back down or backtrack on their words. Since many gaslighters are narcissists, they are accustomed to lying and doing it without any shame or fear of getting caught. Don't ever expect them to admit they are lying and apologize for their actions. They will instead point the finger at you and tell you that it is all in your head, you imagine things, this never happened, or you are losing your mind. Even if you show them a video or audio of themselves to prove they are lying, they will tell you that you heard it wrong, this audio isn't real, or these things were taken out of context. Deep down, you may feel that they are lying, but the gaslighter can be very persuasive and keep coming up with more lies to support their original lie, making it impossible to argue with them or contradict them. Eventually, self-doubt starts sneaking in, and you begin to second-guess yourself.

Why does a gaslighter continue lying even when they are caught? The answer is simple they know it will work. Any normal human being will find this behavior confusing. Normal people don't continue to lie, especially when they are caught. Gaslighters want to confuse their victims and weaken their defenses. Eventually, you will only remember their lies and fabricated stories instead of the truth and the facts you discovered. A gaslighter's goal is to control you. They keep lying to create a false narrative, make you believe their reality, and question yours. Instead of arguing with the gaslighter every time you suspect they are lying, you'll remember all the times the gaslighter proved you wrong. Eventually, the victim will accept everything their abuser tells them to. If they believe something is wrong, they will doubt themselves and question their sanity rather than confront the abuser.

Exaggerating

Exaggeration is quite similar to lying and is another trait of a gaslighter. Marketing agencies employ this tactic when advertising a brand. Brands rarely stick with the truth about what their products do. They tend to exaggerate and manipulate the truth. They promise you the perfect body, hair, or skin using photoshopped images or celebrities who have had plastic surgery to make you believe that this is what you will look like once you use their products. Individuals do the same thing, but instead of selling a product, they exaggerate to sell themselves.

When the gaslighter is a narcissist, exaggeration is their tool to keep their fake image intact. They exaggerate their qualities and abilities to make themselves look good. For instance, they may exaggerate things about their career, social life, or love life to lift themselves up and appear superior. You may find the gaslighter showing off, bragging about things that didn't happen, or using other self-aggrandizement tactics. Their goal isn't only to appear superior but also to make others feel inferior. Exaggeration is also how the gaslighter distorts the victim's reality. They create a false narrative through lying and exaggeration to confuse their victims. Everything is bigger and more complicated than it should be, and nothing is simple. Exaggeration can be very frustrating for the victim since nothing is as it seems. All their statements, stories, and characteristics are exaggerated. Nothing is real, genuine, or straightforward with a gaslighter; everything is exaggerated.

Refusing to Admit Flaws

If you wait for a gaslighter to admit their flaws, then you'll wait forever. You have to understand that gaslighters aren't confident individuals, which is why they want to control the people in their lives rather than be their true selves and treat others with love and kindness. These people don't have thick skins, which is why they can't handle it when someone calls them out on their harmful behavior or lies. To illustrate the difference - when you confront a normal person with their flaws, they will often listen to you and try to understand how their actions may have hurt your feelings. They will acknowledge their flaws and promise to change or to be careful to avoid causing you further pain. However, the gaslighter will not accept your "accusations." In their own minds, these people see themselves as perfect beings who don't have any flaws, and when you confront them, you threaten the grandiose image they have created for themselves. Their fragile ego prevents them from admitting their flaws or acknowledging them. They live in their distorted reality where they see themselves as perfect, and everything is other people's fault rather than theirs. They will either act innocent and pretend that they don't understand what you are talking about or get angry or defensive. In order to control you, the manipulator has to deny their flaws, so you are unable to hold anything against them.

Becoming Aggressive When Criticized

Since gaslighters have thin skin, they will not take criticism kindly and often get angry and aggressive. Expect an angry tantrum, a fight, passive aggression, or the gaslighter walking away from you whenever you criticize their behavior. Regular people accept criticism and apologize for their actions. On the other hand, a gaslighter will escalate the issue by doubling down on the criticism or intimidating you, so you will think twice before criticizing them again. Gaslighters have a different view when it comes to relationships. They don't see people as partners or equals. Everything is a competition. Someone has to be a loser for the other to be the winner. When you criticize them, you put them in a position where they can be the loser, which is unacceptable, and they will lash out or blame you for their actions rather than accept your criticism.

Getting aggressive is their way of manipulating you so you won't criticize them again or comment on their actions. This tactic is meant to scare you from ever speaking up or pointing out how the gaslighter's actions are hurting you. Next time they do something that bothers or hurts you, you will think twice before saying anything. You don't want to upset the gaslighter, so you bottle up your feelings instead. This gives the gaslighter the chance to do whatever they want, knowing that their victim will remain silent because they are either afraid or don't want to risk upsetting the gaslighter. As a result, the gaslighter will keep abusing the victim to exert their control without ever getting called out for their actions.

False Image Projection

Gaslighters often project an idealized image of themselves to the world. This is the result of their low self-esteem and insecurities. They don't want anyone to see them for who they really are, so they hide their true selves behind a false image. This image gives them power over their victims as they use it to hide their insecurities and only showcase their best qualities. This idealized image is often of someone dominant and an alpha male or female. They keep up this image in all areas of their lives, whether it's their job, personal life, or relationship. Gaslighters who work in politics and the media usually create a grandiose image of themselves to brainwash and control a group of people and influence their opinions and decisions. A perfect example of this is a former U.S. president. He believed that he was smart and even a genius because he won the election on his first try. He even mentioned on more than one occasion that he was a smart person. There is a reason that his supporters believe that he was the best president this country has ever seen. They fell for the image he created for himself.

Gaslighters often view themselves as powerful, successful, and strong. They can be extremely cruel towards people they deem weak and see as insignificant. They believe that these people deserve their fate and are often proud of themselves when they marginalize them. In order to control their victims, gaslighters view them as weak individuals, and since they have no sympathy for them, it will make the manipulation and control that much easier. They will attack their victims remorselessly. Their attacks can be subtle or direct. The gaslighter has no empathy whatsoever and often feels pleased with themselves when they break someone's spirit. They want their victim to be completely submissive. In time, the image they create for themselves becomes a vital part of their fake identity. It becomes their main personality, replacing their insecure self, which is who they really are. This is why they get aggressive and lash out when someone criticizes the image they have worked so hard to create.

Violating Boundaries

Boundaries protect you from toxic people like gaslighters and narcissists. Your boundaries are how you tell people what behavior you accept and what behavior you won't tolerate. Gaslighters don't like boundaries as they prevent them from getting what they want. Instead of respecting boundaries set by individuals or societies, the gaslighter sees them as a challenge that they must conquer. When a gaslighter succeeds in breaking the rules or violating social norms, they often feel joy and pride in themselves. You will find the gaslighter often testing boundaries to see if they can succeed in breaking someone's self-esteem. A gaslighter will shame or humiliate their victims privately and publicly, mock you or make sarcastic comments about you, or use hateful speech against individuals or groups. They can also be internet trolls, provoking people online just to get attention and feel superior.

Normal individuals respect other people's boundaries because they don't have the sense of entitlement gaslighters have. Violating boundaries is how they dehumanize and oppress their victims. However, their ego and narrow view of the world prevent them from seeing how disrespectful and damaging their behavior can be. Gaslighters can take this behavior so far as to commit acts of sexual harassment, hate crimes, financial abuse, and domestic abuse. They don't feel any guilt or shame over their actions. On the contrary, they are often proud of themselves and their superiority. The lack of boundaries makes them easy victims targets for manipulators. They want to take down their victim's defense so they can manipulate them and exert complete control.

Emotional Invalidation

Unlike physical abuse, emotional abuse doesn't leave a mark on your body. However, this doesn't make it any less damaging; in fact, it's this unseen damage that is the most upsetting and dangerous to a victim. Gaslighters enjoy making people suffer, and emotional abuse is the way to do it. These people are consumed by negativity, whether it is in their thoughts or emotions. They get pleasure from arousing emotional pain in their victims and spreading their hate and negativity. They know that this will make the victim feel off-balanced and insecure, which, in turn, feeds the gaslighter's need for power. They will invalidate your priorities, thoughts, and feelings without feeling any guilt for all the pain and suffering they put their victims through. As mentioned, when you criticize or confront the gaslighter with their mistakes, they will get aggressive and angry rather than validate your feelings. Instead of acknowledging their mistakes, they will blame you for their actions. For instance, they will tell you that they yelled at you because you weren't listening or that they got angry because you provoked them.

Gaslighters are unpredictable. You never know how they are going to react. They have severe mood swings, and they can make a scene out of a simple situation. They will make victims feel as if they are walking on eggshells around them because they don't know how the gaslighter will react or what will set them off. If the gaslighter feels that you are taking back your power or standing up for yourself, they will break your spirit and lower your self-esteem, so you lose your confidence and go back to being under their control. Gaslighters expect their victims to be at their beck and call, agree with them on everything, and rise to their expectations. If you fail to do what is expected of you, you will become agitated and aggressive. They want to make you feel inferior and dependent on them to boost their egos.

Coercion

Coercion is another trait that helps the gaslighter control others. It is when they physically, mentally, and emotionally abuse their victims. They also isolate the victim from their loved ones, so they will have no one else to rely on but the abuser. The gaslighter controls every aspect of the victim's life, including where they go, who they hang out with, what they wear, and how they spend their time. They do this while constantly humiliating and making degrading comments about their victims. Coercion is a power move intended to manipulate the victim emotionally. Gaslighters don't have the emotional maturity or sympathy to understand their partner's needs, have an open discussion about their problems, compromise for the other person's sake, or handle not getting what they want. Coercive control is their best option. The victim becomes a prisoner, and the gaslighter is the prison guard. The victim can't do anything until they get permission from their abuser.

Controlling Others

The main goal behind gaslighting is to control their victims. They will manipulate the victim and make them question and second guess themselves, becoming totally reliant on their emotional captor. As the victim begins to doubt themselves, they lose their confidence and trust in their ability to make any decisions concerning their lives. This gives the gaslighter the opening they crave to be in full control and make decisions for you that will only benefit them. Whether the gaslighter is a politician, someone close to you, or the media, they psychologically manipulate their victims' reality by distorting the truth to reduce their confidence and make them question themselves. They go to the extent of telling their victims what to think and how they should feel. Simply put, they set rules for the victim to live by, and if they break these rules or disagree with the abuser, they can become angry and hostile. The gaslighter is enraged and terrified to see the victim getting powerful and gaining control over their lives. This is why they lash out whenever the victim breaks the rules they set for them.

Gaslighters are extremely weak and insecure individuals. Although they seem charming and confident on the outside, what's inside is a whole different story. Deep down, they feel powerless and know they can't have a normal relationship or even a normal interaction without manipulation and gaslighting. In reality, these individuals have no power over you; they just manipulate you into believing that they do. When they feel like they are no longer in control, they show their fear in the form of anger. They will never admit to their weakness or let you see through them. They are very protective of the image they have created for themselves. All these traits show how twisted and unstable a gaslighter is. They are unable to express themselves using normal human emotions. Gaslighters can't sympathize, feel other people's pain, or put themselves in other's shoes. All they know is lies, manipulation, and emotional abuse.

Chapter 7

Gaslighting Methods

Gaslighters are very smart individuals. They will never be straightforward or tell you directly what they want from you. Don't expect a gaslighter to show you their cards right away. They play the long game by taking their time to exert their control. A gaslighter will start small and test your boundaries first. They don't want you to suspect their intentions right away or to feel that something isn't right. There is a reason gaslighters are good at what they do and often succeed in manipulating their victims. They use very specific techniques, and it can be hard or even impossible for the victim to guess that they are being manipulated. Seeing as gaslighters seem like sincere individuals with good intentions at first, it can be hard to believe these people mean you harm. However, they say and do things while intending totally different things.

The intent behind the methods the gaslighter uses is to emotionally manipulate you. They want you to question your reality and sanity and second-guess yourself until eventually your self-esteem and self-worth are completely destroyed. These methods are usually used by narcissists, dictators, cult leaders, and abusive individuals to control the people in their lives and get them to do what they want. Gaslighters don't just act recklessly, they have a strategy, and they take their time with it.

You may have heard about it in the news or seen people in your life being brainwashed. You probably wonder how it's possible for someone to give up everything they believe in, including their identity, and relinquish all control to someone else. But gaslighters use very powerful and effective techniques to confuse and wear their victims down. The victims are often defenseless and unaware of what they are subjected to. Charles Manson and even the terrorist group Isis are a few examples of individuals who use gaslighting techniques to manipulate the masses and take advantage of them.

You may not realize it, but you or someone you love may be the victim of gaslighting. Recognizing the manipulators' methods will help you identify this behavior and take the necessary steps immediately.

Distorting Reality

Distorting your reality is a very powerful and damaging tactic that gaslighters use to make their victims believe their lies. This technique was the main concept demonstrated in the "Gaslight" movie. The wife could clearly see the lights flickering, but her husband manipulated her to such an extent that she believed her reality wasn't true, and she believed she was losing her mind. If you listen to the song "It wasn't me" by Shaggy, you probably think that it is a fun song with a cool beat and catchy lyrics. However, listen to this song again and pay attention to the lyrics. The song is the perfect example of gaslighting behavior through distorting reality. The lyrics say: "She even caught me on camera (wasn't me), she saw the marks on my shoulder (wasn't me), and heard the words that I told her (wasn't me)." Even though the girl saw him cheating with her own eyes, caught him on camera, and had proof, he still denied it was him. This is classic reality distortion where the manipulator wants their victim to believe a false narrative instead of what they see with their own eyes.

In psychology, there is a phenomenon that is referred to as the "illusory truth effect." It's when you believe something that is clearly untrue because it has been repeated to you over and over again. Simply put, a person will believe a lie if the abuser keeps repeating it to them. This is why some people believe rumors or fake news; since it is spread widely and they keep finding it in different sources, they will believe it, even if the news seems irrational or unbelievable. If the source is someone or something familiar to you, like a loved one or a trusted news source, you will most likely believe what they are saying, no matter how ridiculous it sounds. For most people, familiarity triumphs over irrationality.

A gaslighter will rewrite your reality and change your history using the illusory truth effect. They will repeat lies so often that they eventually become truths that the victim can't deny. Eventually, these lies negate your own true experience, distort your reality, and make you question your perception and second-guess yourself.

Example

The perfect example of this method is the husband in the "Gaslight" movie. He kept repeating lies to his wife and denying certain facts, like telling her that the lights weren't flickering. Even though she could see with her own eyes that the lights were flickering, she believed her husband because he kept repeating the same lie until she believed it to be true. He made her question her perceptions and reality until she believed that there was something wrong with her and that she shouldn't leave the house.

Isolation

In order for a gaslighter to control their victims, they must first isolate them from their support system. Although it can be hard for you to identify gaslighting behavior when it is happening to you, a trusted friend or family member could either recognize that you are being manipulated or feel that something isn't right. Remember, the gaslighter wants you to only depend on them, so having other people in your life who support you or lift you up will make it hard for the abuser to destroy your self-esteem. Having your friends and family by your side is the gaslighter's worst nightmare. If a friend notices the abuser's manipulative behavior, they will point it out to you and help you walk away from this toxic relationship. This is why the gaslighter will slowly and gradually isolate you from the people you love.

The abuser will spend most of their time with you, so you won't have time to see your friends and tell you, "Your friends or family don't like me" or "Your friends aren't happy for us." They may also tell you lies about the people you love, fabricating stories that your friends are jealous of you or they don't want to see you happy. They will refuse to attend any social gatherings with you, such as friends' birthdays or family dinners, and when they do, they can be rude to your loved ones. If you happen to go out with friends, they will call you every hour and get aggressive when you don't answer your phone or text them right away. Meanwhile, they will make themselves seem like the only person you can trust and rely on. Isolation from your support system makes you vulnerable and easy to manipulate or control. You will have no one by your side to open your eyes to the abuse or raise your self-esteem whenever the abuser breaks your spirit.

Example

You make plans to see your friends, and you're very excited about it because you haven't seen them in a while. You tell your gaslighter partner, and they make you feel guilty about it. They will turn the tables and accuse you of not wanting to spend time with them or that you only care about your friends. The truth is that you, in fact, spend most of your time with your partner and rarely see your friends or family. In time, you begin feeling guilty for spending any time with other people and dedicate all your free time to your partner to please them.

Using What Is Dear to You as Ammunition

Gaslighters study their victims to learn their weaknesses and see what they can use against them. Whether it is your children, pets, career, family, friends, or identity, the gaslighter will attack anything or anyone who is important to you or use them as a bargaining chip. This technique can be very painful and damaging to the victim's spirit and mental health. It is one thing to mess with you, but it is a whole other thing when it comes to the people you care about or your career. This can rock you to the core and make you feel off-balanced, which is what the gaslighter wants.

Example

You love your job so much and work hard to have a long and fulfilling career. Your gaslighter boss knows that your job is very important to you. Instead of supporting you and helping you advance in your career, your boss manipulates you into second-guessing yourself and questioning whether you are good enough for your job. Your boss may do this by only giving you negative feedback and making you feel that you can easily be replaced. Their goal is to shake your confidence and make you unaware of your self-worth.

Name-Calling

One of the gaslighters' goals is to destroy their victim's self-esteem, and name-calling is an effective method that can help the gaslighter achieve their goal. Gaslighters only feel superior when they have brought their victims down and made them feel completely inferior. They learn your insecurities and bring them up by using name-calling whenever you are feeling down. If their victim has self-esteem issues, this can make their job much easier as they will easily be affected by name-calling. Unlike a confident person who is aware of who they are and believes in themselves and their abilities, a person with low self-esteem will believe and internalize whatever the gaslighter calls them and eventually consider their words part of their own identity.

Understand that a normal and healthy person will never resort to name-calling. Even if the gaslighter tries to make it seem they have good intentions, their intent is always malicious. It can be a parent who knows you are insecure about your body and keep bringing your weight into every conversation, or your boss who knows that you are afraid of failure and keeps reminding you every time you lose a deal. The more they keep repeating these words, the easier it will be for you to believe them. This is meant to make you feel unlovable and unworthy, so you believe that no one else will tolerate you but your partner or parent or that no other place will hire you, so you put up with the abuse.

Example

Your ex-partner cheated on you, and your new partner knows how this has affected you and left you extremely insecure about your looks. Whenever you gain weight or leave the house without makeup, your partner makes hurtful comments like, "Are you going to leave the house looking like that? You look like a homeless person," "Put some makeup on; you look like a zombie," or "Did you dress like that when you were with your ex? You look ten years older. No wonder they cheated on you." Whenever you broach the subject that their words are hurtful, they'll say you are just being oversensitive, or they just want you to take care of yourself, so they won't cheat on you like your ex-partner.

Love Bombing

Love bombing usually occurs in romantic relationships. This method involves praise, flattery, gifts, and over-the-top romance and affection. It can sometimes be hard to spot because you want to believe that this person is genuine and what they are doing is merely a sweet gesture because they really like you. However, if someone seems like they are too good to be true, it's because they really are. This tactic is a favorite of narcissistic gaslighters. This is how they get your attention, so you eventually fall for them and come under their control.

That said, their "sweet gestures" aren't what they seem, and deep down, you may feel that something isn't right. For instance, they might buy an expensive gift. This can seem like normal behavior, but the gaslighter makes sure to let you know how much the gift costs. They want you to know how much they spend on you, so you feel indebted to them. They will continuously remind you of all the good things they did for you, so, in turn, you won't be able to say no to them and do everything they want. This isn't how normal relationships work; you don't give something and expect something else in return. However, love bombing is how the gaslighters manipulate their victims. Even their compliments are meant to mold you into a certain image. The "love bombing" stage is also meant to confuse the victim. When their mask finally slips, and you begin to see them for who they truly are, you feel confused and unable to leave because you remember who they were at first and the "sweet gestures" and charming personality they showed you when you first met.

Love bombing in any relationship is a red flag. If you feel that too much is happening at once, then you are in the love bombing stage of being manipulated by a gaslighter. Remember that normal and healthy relationships move at a much slower pace, so you don't feel overwhelmed. You usually connect with someone first, learn about each other, and then go from there. However, this person shows you adoration in no time. Although this usually takes place in romantic relationships, "love bombing" can occur in other relationships as well. Someone you just met can call you their best friend, or your boss keeps telling you that you are their favorite employee when you have only been in the company for three days.

Example

You meet someone, and they seem nice, attentive, and charming at first. After the second date, they tell you they love you. They post your pictures all over social media while expressing their undying love for you. They shower you with physical affection that can seem too much and make others uncomfortable whenever you are in public. When you tell them to slow things down, they will say things like "I love you, and I can't help myself" or "You are so amazing, and I want to show the whole world how lucky I am."

Rally People against You

Seeing that gaslighters want to make you question your sanity, they may need to rally other people to their side. If they keep telling you that you imagine things or are going crazy, but your friends or family tell you otherwise, their plan won't work. This is why a gaslighter isolates the victim from their loved ones. However, in some cases, rather than removing you from your support system, they will turn it against you. They may tell people that you drink too much, your behavior is erratic, you are losing your mind, or you imagine things. They may even say things in front of others to confuse you to show them that you have a problem. The gaslighter will tell people they are concerned about you and your well-being. They will pretend that they feel helpless and don't know what to do about their strange behavior. This will get others to sympathize with them, and they will begin telling you that your drinking is getting out of control or that you should seek psychiatric help.

This tactic will also make you feel isolated and alone as everyone in your life keeps questioning your sanity until you begin to believe that there is something wrong with you. Consequently, whenever you complain about the abuser, no one in your circle will believe you. They already think that you are the problem or that you need help. Eventually, you will begin to believe the same, which will make it easy for the abuser to control you.

Example

You are having dinner with your partner, and you drink wine with your meal. Your partner tells you not to drink too much because you lose your temper when you do. You look confused and tell your partner that you only have one or two drinks at dinner, and you rarely ever get drunk. They tell you that your sister and your best friend agree that you have a drinking problem. You feel even more confused and decide to stop drinking altogether because you fear your drinking may hurt other people's feelings. However, in reality, you have never had a drinking problem and only drink occasionally. Your partner told the people in your life a different story that made them worry about you.

It is a mistake to believe that you are immune to gaslighting behavior. You probably read all these tactics and thought that this can only happen to weak people or that you are too smart to fall for this type of manipulation. However, it isn't an exaggeration to say that some gaslighters are geniuses and are really good at what they do. All these tactics are done gradually and over time. It doesn't matter how smart or aware you are; you can still fall for their tricks. Since they take their time, you may not be aware of what is happening until it's too late and you've fallen prey to their manipulation.

Their whole purpose is to confuse you so you won't be able to withstand them. You will feel that this isn't happening to you and that you're living in a twilight zone. Nothing feels right or real, but you don't know what to do about it. They will wear you down, sap your energy, and make you feel alone. However, there are ways you can protect yourself from gaslighting and stand up to them. You can save yourself, which is what you will learn about in the next chapter.

Chapter 8

Avoiding Gaslighters

Now that you have learned about gaslighters, their motives, traits, and methods, you probably wonder if avoiding these people and their toxic behavior is possible. Gaslighters are master manipulators who thrive on chaos. It can take a very long time to recover from the damage they cause to your mental and emotional health. The entire experience can destroy your identity to the point where you become a shell of what you used to be. You look in the mirror and don't recognize the face staring back at you. Although your features are the same, something is different. This is what gaslighting does to you, but it is still possible to save yourself and find your way back to your old self.

Signs You Are a Victim of Gaslighting

If you still aren't sure whether or not you are being gaslit, then, instead of looking at the gaslighter and their behavior, take a look at yourself. You will be able to feel the impact of gaslighting on your mental and emotional health. Deep down, you feel that something isn't right. If you are a victim, you'll always feel confused, and you don't know what's real and what isn't anymore. Your life feels surreal and out of control. You feel helpless and don't know what to do to get back to normal. Remember that your job, family, friendships, and relationships should make you feel better about yourself, or at the very least, not make you feel worse. However, if someone in your life leaves you confused, frustrated, and drained after every interaction, you should question their intentions.

Certain signs you should look out for will help you determine if you are a victim of gaslighting.

Self-Doubt

It is normal to experience self-doubt every once in a while. Even the most confident and smartest people doubt themselves on occasion. However, if the feeling is persistent enough to be overwhelming, you may be a victim of gaslighting.

Second-Guessing Yourself

You can have disagreements or fights with people in your life. Sometimes they can be in the wrong, and there are times when you will need to confront your actions to see if they are hurting others. However, if you always find yourself in the wrong while the other person is playing the victim, then something isn't right here. When confronting the gaslighter, you will end up feeling confused, second-guessing yourself, and questioning your sanity. If you don't trust yourself or your recollection of certain events, you may question the person making you feel this way instead of questioning your sanity.

Low Self-Esteem

No one should make you feel less or remind you of your insecurities just to feel good about themselves. If you have been feeling less confident lately, it's time for some introspection to ask yourself who or what is making you feel this way. People shouldn't bring up your insecurities or remind you of your past mistakes in normal conversations. This isn't healthy behavior.

Feeling on Edge

Living with a gaslighter can make you feel as if you are living on a knife's edge. This is someone who has convinced you - and others that you are losing your mind and has made you question your judgment and perceptions. As a result, you feel like you're reeling and don't feel normal anymore.

Emotional Distress

Seeing that gaslighters isolate their victims or turn the people in their lives against them, you will end up feeling alone and emotionally distressed. Mood swings, anxiety, fear, high blood pressure, heart palpitations, and even depression are all signs that you are distressed. Remember, normal relationships shouldn't make you feel this way.

Making Excuses

Are you constantly making excuses for your partner, sibling, or parent to the people in your life? Since gaslighters will never own up to their actions or apologize for their behavior, you will find yourself making excuses for them or lying on their behalf. Lying to your loved ones can feel exhausting and alienate you from them, which is precisely what the gaslighter wants.

Constantly Apologizing

If every argument or fight with someone ends up with you saying, "I am sorry," then you are dealing with a gaslighter. You will find yourself apologizing even though you did nothing wrong, but you just want to keep the peace and avoid angering the other person. It doesn't make sense for every problem to be your fault. This means that someone is manipulating you to avoid taking responsibility for your actions.

Walking on Eggshells

Walking on eggshells and feeling afraid that you may say or do the wrong thing and anger someone is not a way to live your life. This means that the gaslighter has made you believe something is wrong with you. You will find yourself living your life only to make this person happy, even if it is at your expense. Living in fear and denial isn't normal, and no one should make you live this way.

Who Am I?

Do you feel like yourself? Do you feel as if you have lost control of your life? Does someone in your life or a relationship feel off, but you can't pinpoint an exact reason? These are all strong signs that you are a victim of gaslighting. It doesn't matter how strong, confident, or smart you are; you can still lose yourself to a gaslighter. The most obvious sign that you are a victim of gaslighting is feeling unlike yourself.

What to Do

If you think you are a victim of gaslighting, there are things that you need to do to get out of this situation. One of the most common things a gaslighter does is make you question your memory and replace it with a false narrative. Instead of taking what the gaslighter says at face value or fighting with them, you can simply say; that clearly, you both have different recollections of the events, so there is no need to have an argument or a debate about it. This will prevent the gaslighter from controlling the narrative or making you second-guess yourself. Standing your ground without pointing fingers or allowing someone to make you feel guilty may be your best option here.

Another thing a gaslighter does is that they never acknowledge or validate your feelings. Don't allow anyone to tell you how you should feel. Stand your ground and stay true to your feelings. Tell the gaslighter that even if they don't feel the same way, they still can't dictate how you should feel. Understand that there is nothing wrong with any feelings you are experiencing and own them.

The gaslighter may make you question things about yourself. For instance, they may tell you that you have a drinking problem or that you exaggerate things because you love drama. Again, don't accept what they are saying at face value. Have a talk with your trusted circle and tell them what happened. Get their opinion and see if they will reinforce your perception. Talking to someone you trust can help validate your feelings and distinguish between what is real and what isn't. Having people you trust in your life can give you the support you need. Don't allow anyone to isolate you from your loved ones.

How to Stop Being Manipulated by a Gaslighter

Recognize Gaslighting Behavior

The first thing you should do to stop the manipulation is to recognize that it is happening. The information provided in this book is a good start. The second thing you should watch out for is certain phrases like:

- You are too sensitive

- You are over dramatic

- You are making things up

- You are exaggerating

- You are crazy. This has never happened

Recognizing gaslighting behavior is key to helping you break the cycle of abuse.

Keep a Journal

As mentioned, the gaslighter wants to make you question yourself and your sanity. Keeping a journal and writing down your interactions with them and your recollection of events will help you protect your truth. Make it a habit to go back to your journal every time the gaslighter makes you question your perception, provides a false narrative or makes you feel that you are losing your mind. This will also help you keep confident in yourself and stop doubting your sanity.

Be Defiant

Trust your story and your recollection of events. Don't allow them to rewrite your story, no matter what the gaslighter says. By now, you are aware of their tactics and their intentions, so be defiant and trust your version of reality. You know your truth, resist, and don't allow them to alter events. They may call you difficult just because you choose to resist, but you know what they are and remaining defiant is how you will protect yourself.

Know Your Purpose

Having a conversation with a gaslighter can be exhausting and draining. Not only are these people experts in manipulation, but they treat every conversation as a win or lose. Knowing your purpose before having a conversation with a gaslighter will keep the conversation simple. They will deflect and distract you, so keep in mind the main points you want to talk about in advance. Remember, gaslighters are liars who will never acknowledge or validate your feelings, so don't expect this from them. When you know your purpose, you will remain focused on the issue you are discussing and will prevent them from taking the conversation in a different direction.

End the Conversation

You may enter the conversation knowing your purpose, but the gaslighter will use their manipulative tactics. You will find yourself going around in circles, unable to settle things, and even finding that the conversation has been taken in a completely different direction than the one you wanted. If you find that whatever you are saying falls on deaf ears and the gaslighter insists on minimizing your feelings or distorting your reality, then simply walk away from the conversation. Remember that you are your own person, and you have the freedom to leave a conversation going nowhere. Ending a conversation will also prevent the gaslighter from manipulating you any further and making you second-guess yourself or question your sanity.

As mentioned, gaslighters are very smart individuals. Outsmarting a gaslighter isn't as easy as you think. However, the best way to deal with them is by disengaging and ending the conversation. Even if you treat the conversation like an investigation and provide proof, the gaslighter will still deny and deflect. They are pros, and sometimes it can be difficult to win with them. End the conversation and simply walk away.

Tell Them How You Feel

Not all gaslighters are aware of their behavior. Having a conversation with them about their actions and how they are making you feel may help. Explain to them their toxic behavior and give them specific incidents of how their actions made you feel. This will only work if the gaslighter doesn't know what they are doing and doesn't have any bad intentions. They may want to get help and change their ways to stop hurting and abusing the people they care about.

However, if they resist and deflect, then they are aware of what they are doing, and this conversation will be futile. This is especially true if the gaslighter is also a narcissist. In this case, having a conversation about your feelings with them will take you nowhere, drain you, and make you feel worse. So give it a chance and tell them how you feel, but if they resort to their typical manipulative ways, walk away.

Leave

You can try everything with the gaslighter, but nothing changes. The damage done through gaslighting is severe. Your mental health, who you are, your relationships, and everything you love about yourself is vulnerable to attack. Your best option under these circumstances is to seriously consider leaving the gaslighter. If the gaslighter is your partner, end the relationship with them. Some gaslighters throw frighteningly angry tantrums when they are enraged. That can put you in danger. Ending the relationship will end the cycle of abuse and protect you from harm's way. This step is going to be hard, especially if you are in love with them, but it can be the best thing to do for your well-being. If the gaslighter is a parent or family member, who it will be hard to cut contact with, then limit your contact with them and set healthy boundaries. If the gaslighter is a friend, then either cut them off or set boundaries with them, and if it's your boss, consider looking for a new job.

The Effects of Being a Victim of Gaslighting

There are short-term and long-term effects to being a victim of gaslighting. The short-term effects are usually subtle because they happen to you at the beginning of your relationship with the abuser. This is the stage when their manipulation tactics are small, and they conceal them as jokes or pretend that they are genuinely concerned about you. The short-term effects include feeling tense, irritable, unable to focus, and frustrated as a result of constant fights or arguments. You will also have friends or family members come to you with concerns about your well-being.

Gaslighters play the long game, and the more time you spend with them, the more severe the effects will be. As a result of having your reality distorted and your sanity questioned, you will begin to believe that you have a mental health disorder. Naturally, this will affect your mental health. You will begin to feel constantly anxious, and it will keep getting worse. Your life will not be your own as you will depend on the gaslighter for everything, and you will be under their control. This will lead you to feel depressed and isolated from your loved ones. In some severe cases, gaslighting can lead to physical abuse and domestic violence.

You will also experience:

- Insecurity
- Self-doubt
- Low self-esteem
- Anxiety
- Trauma
- PTSD symptoms
- Depression

Setting Boundaries

Setting boundaries is how you can protect yourself against toxic people. Your boundaries will protect you and help you take care of yourself and your well-being. They are necessary, especially if you have to interact with a toxic person.

Identify Your Boundaries

Identifying your boundaries will help you settle on what type of behavior you will not tolerate under any circumstances. This will empower you to know that you will not accept certain behaviors and will walk away if others don't respect your boundaries. It will also start the long process of getting your confidence back.

Communicate Your Boundaries

Identify your boundaries, and communicate them in a clear and calm manner. Take a deep breath and simply tell others what behavior you will not tolerate. Remember, you don't owe anyone an explanation, and you don't need to give excuses as to why you feel the way you do. So don't be defensive, over-explain, or point the finger and blame. It is vital that you remain calm, especially if the gaslighter has just triggered you. Stay on point and focus on communicating your boundaries rather than your feelings toward the gaslighter.

Social Media

Social media lacks boundaries. There is no privacy, and people share intimate details about their lives, giving others the chance to comment on their lives or bully them. Setting boundaries on social media won't only protect you from gaslighters but will protect your mental health as well since social media can be a toxic place. Unfriend, unfollow, or mute anyone on social media who tries to cross your boundaries.

Change Takes Time

Don't expect the gaslighter to begin respecting your boundaries right away. It is going to take them some time to understand why you set these boundaries and adjust. However, remain firm about your boundaries and make it clear that they aren't negotiable.

Disrespecting Boundaries

Gaslighters enjoy testing and violating other people's boundaries; it's what feeds their needs. Expect them to disrespect your boundaries, so be prepared to take action right away. First, decide which of your boundaries are essential and non-negotable and which aren't. There may be things you can compromise on, so decide what you are willing to accept. However, this is your decision. Don't make compromises because someone else expects you to; compromise because you want to. Your needs are important. Don't compromise on things that will please others at your expense. When it comes to your non-negotiable boundaries, stand by them and make it clear that nothing the gaslighter will do or say will change your mind.

Some people will not accept your boundaries, no matter what you say or do. This can be hard to accept, but you will have to decide whether you want this person in your life or not. In this case, you will need to stop interacting with the gaslighter.

How to Stop Interaction with the Gaslighter

As has been stated, sometimes your only option is to leave the gaslighter. You can either limit your contact with them or cut them off. Understanding that limiting or stopping your contact isn't cruel, even if the gaslighter makes you feel this way is crucial to the success of your first steps to freedom. You are doing this to protect yourself. Some friends or family members may guilt you into contacting the gaslighter, especially if it is a parent or a family member that you have to cut off. They don't understand what you have been through and how vital this choice is to your protection. Don't listen to anyone who doesn't know your story or allow them to make you feel guilty or pressure you to talk to the gaslighter one last time. You have already said everything you wanted to say and mentioned how essential your boundaries are, but they didn't listen, so having another conversation is futile.

Block them on all social media platforms, stop answering their calls, and don't attend events they will be invited to. They may send you messages via friends or ask them to help you get back together. Be firm and tell friends or family that you will not discuss this person anymore. If they bring the gaslighter up, leave, so they know you are serious. Remember, the abuser will not tell you anything new, and all their words are lies, and all their promises are empty.

Naturally, there will be moments when you will be tempted to talk to them or answer their calls, especially if this is someone that you care about or have a history with. Talk to your loved ones about how you feel, and they will be more than happy to remind you of how bad things were and that you are now better off.

There is no denying how toxic gaslighting is, but there is a way out. Don't hesitate to limit your contact with the gaslighter or cut them off if necessary. Make your mental health and well-being a priority and take a stand against toxic behavior.

Chapter 9

Escaping Manipulation

Now that you have learned all you need to know about the different types and tactics of dark psychology and gaslighting, it's time to find out how to protect yourself. This chapter will explain how you can escape the extension to gaslighting - manipulation - by fighting back against it and protecting yourself from it. Then, you will learn how to set healthy personal boundaries.

Fight Back against Manipulation

Standing up to a manipulator is not the easiest thing to do. They're very careful not to let you become aware of their tactics. Fortunately, there are some psychological games you, too, can play to effectively fight back against manipulation.

Close Any Entryways

The first step to fighting back against any manipulator is to close all your entryways. In other words, don't give them a way in. In most cases, a manipulator will use a specific situation as leverage to exploit you whenever they need to. For instance, they may do you a favor, and even if you've never called it in, they can get you to do something you don't want to do later. They may offer to set you up with a job, buy you dinner, or give you a gift. This way, when they ask you to babysit their child or fill in for them at work, you won't be able to say no. The situation is different from one person to the next. So, take the time to think about your manipulator's motives, tools, or tactics. Whatever you do, don't fall for their tricks. Decline the job interview they offered to get you, explain that you have dinner plans, or return the gift that they gave you.

Use Their Name

Did you know that calling someone by their name can make them more pleasant to deal with? It also facilitates understanding between people. While this may not get them completely off your back, addressing your manipulator with their name can make them generally friendlier. If they have nicknames, make sure to use the version of their name that they like the most.

Make Eye Contact

This psychological trick can help you throw them off their game. If you've dealt with a manipulator before, you know that a simple "no" will not always do the trick. They know how to get what they want and won't settle until they get their way. Don't worry, though. You should be fine as long as you look them in the eye and stand your ground. Manipulators have a strong, intense gaze. It's one of their games. So beat them at it and hold the eye contact until they feel uncomfortable.

Shift the Attention to Them

Manipulators are masters at playing the victim. They also know how to turn the tables and shift the blame, which is why they never expect you to question them at all. All you need to do to throw a manipulator off is to ask them a simple question, putting their intentions to the test. Do they often ask for your opinion and then make you feel dumb for speaking up? If that's the case, you can ask them if they really care about what you have to say since it feels like they're asking just for the sake of asking. You can also ask them if they'll still be able to support you or maintain healthy communication if your opinions or decisions are different from theirs. If the manipulator you're dealing with often makes you feel guilty if you don't take their advice or do things that they ask you to do, you can ask them if they really think you'd do this even though they must realize it's not the best thing for you. It also helps if you give them a taste of their own medicine. The next time your co-worker asks you to do their tasks for them, you can say, "only if you do (a task) for me tomorrow!" They probably won't ask you again.

Reiterate Until They Understand

Have you ever tried repeating a phrase over and over to a manipulator? If so, then you know that it's a surefire way to frustrate them, especially when it isn't something that they wish to hear. Their reaction may have led you to avoid doing so, even when they refuse to understand you. However, repeating the same phrase in an emotionless, monotone is going to get to them. You don't need to think of a long statement that forces you to explain yourself. It can be something as simple as "I don't want to," "I am not having this conversation," or "I'm not going to do it." Most importantly, make sure to keep your emotions in check. Be completely emotionless and keep the same tone. You should make it sound as though you don't care.

Don't Allow Them to Make Generalizations

One of the reasons manipulators succeed is they know how to seep "generalizations" into conversations. Have you ever felt guilty or ashamed because they pointed fingers at you and said, "you always do this!" or "you always behave that way!" They can be at fault and still manage to shift the blame onto you. For instance, they may take your slightly higher voice or "overreaction" out of context and tell you that you're always dramatic, which is why they "can never communicate with you." Say you handed in a task half an hour later than you were supposed to. Your boss then calls you out for never handing things in on time, even though this was your first time.

Don't allow manipulators to generalize behaviors or reactions like these. Instead of getting angry or frustrated, which is something they'll also use against you, you can calmly ask them to provide examples of other times when you acted like this.

Use the Power of Imagination

If someone's manipulating you, the chances are that they want to frustrate you enough to drive you to give way to an undesirable reaction. They'll be able to shift the blame on you once you get angry, raise your voice, or say something that you wouldn't otherwise say. While it may feel stupid at first, this distraction and relaxation technique never fails to work against someone who's trying to manipulate you. Imagine a huge aquarium with very thick walls standing between you and that person. You can't hear anything they have to say. You can see their lips moving, their facial expressions changing, and their hands being waved around. All sound is blocked, so you have no idea what they're saying. Feel free to make a few mental jokes about it!

Maintain Your Personal Space

Manipulative people don't have respect for physical boundaries. They'll get closer to you than you'd like. They may touch your hand or give you an unsolicited pat on the back or shoulder. If you want to maintain your private space (which you should, especially when dealing with a manipulator), take a couple of steps back whenever they approach you. This will help you keep space between you and prevent physical contact. Manipulators know that we are generally more likely to say "yes" when there's little personal space or when physical contact has been established. If you're struggling to maintain a safe distance between you and your manipulator, you can insist on discussing all important matters over text, phone call, or online meeting. This way, you won't feel pressured to give in to their requests. This works best in the professional world.

Practice Self-Awareness

Manipulative tactics succeed when the manipulator manages to make you feel guilty. This is a very common offshoot of the gaslighting/manipulation skill set. Let's take a very common social phenomenon. As parents grow older, they often feel left behind. They start complaining to their children about their health and how lonely they feel. When this happens, the children start feeling guilty about leaving their parents behind. They end up neglecting their jobs, duties, and own families to stay close to their parents. If a person starts making you feel guilty, take a moment to check in with yourself before you automatically agree with their opinion of you. Say you are the child in this situation. How often do you visit your parents? Do you call them often and make sure that they have everything they need? Have you done anything to prove the opposite of what they say? If so, then you shouldn't feel guilty.

How to Protect Yourself from Being Manipulated

Manipulation is everywhere around us. We get manipulated and somewhat brainwashed into supporting certain politicians, purchasing products that we don't really need, doing things for friends and family, performing certain tasks at work, and so on. You've probably even unintentionally manipulated someone to get your way before. It is a very common tactic, which is why we need to learn how to protect ourselves from it.

Tune into Your Feelings

It can sometimes be hard to pick up on manipulation. If you suspect that someone is trying to manipulate you, paying attention to your feelings can be a key indicator of whether someone is trying to take advantage of you. Unless the manipulation process unfolds subconsciously, which is highly unlikely, you will at least feel uncomfortable when dealing with that person. Do you notice yourself getting defensive even though it's against your nature? Perhaps you feel unusually guilty, angry, frustrated, or ashamed. Are they making you feel like you are doing something wrong? Take a step back and process the situation objectively. It's not normal to feel uncomfortable when talking to someone. It is usually a red flag that something doesn't sit right. Once you're aware that you're being manipulated, you can start fighting back.

Be an Active Listener

People practice manipulation techniques and gaslighting tactics when they want others to agree with them and understand their points of view. Being an active listener will allow you to fully grasp what they are saying and build a sound and solid argument, opinion, or response. Being an active listener also allows you to establish a sense of trust, which is something that you need in this situation. Make sure to be an objective listener. This means that you shouldn't allow what they're saying to influence your perspective at all. Give them one of the things they want (hearing them out and understanding their motives) without allowing them to take advantage of you. This should satisfy them and give you the time to present your own perspective based on what they had to say.

Maintain a Firm Stance

Maintain a firm stance, something that is known as frame control. This means that you should create an entirely novel and personal perspective based on your beliefs, values, and experience. You should be fully convinced that your point of view is just as important and valid as your manipulator's (or anyone else's). Stand your ground and maintain your opinion and voice, even when they challenge you with a different perspective. You may feel compelled to agree with them just to get the argument over, to please them, or to emerge as the good one in the story. However, remind yourself that this will only encourage them to do the same thing over and over again. Soon enough, they'll chip away at your self-trust, self-esteem, sense of self, and identity. You need to stay true to yourself and everything that you believe in. If you're feeling overwhelmed by the situation, take a step back and observe. Ask them to carry on this conversation some other time, and step away and cool off whenever you feel they're starting to get to you. A manipulator may intentionally confuse you, so you lose sight of your own stance. In that case, tell them that you need time to absorb and think about what they're saying.

Reflect on Their Words and Validate Their Argument

Manipulators want to make sure that they're heard and very well understood. Pausing to reflect on their words before paraphrasing what they said shows them that you understand. Tell them you believe they have good motives, which is true in many cases. Most manipulators aren't necessarily malevolent. They don't want to hurt you but rather want to influence your opinions, perspectives, and actions. Many people aren't even aware of their own manipulative tendencies. They don't realize that the way they communicate with people, especially when asking for favors or presenting an idea or point of view, is considered manipulative. This will require a lot of tolerance and work on your side because if you don't genuinely believe that they may not be ill-intended, you will inevitably become defensive. This makes it harder to win an argument against a manipulator.

Present Your Case

Take a moment to think about this: does the manipulator always know your point of view? When we're aware that we may be dealing with a manipulative person, we often forget to present our position properly. We are too busy trying to protect ourselves, forgetting that maybe the other person really doesn't know what our perspective is. Avoid being critical of what they say. Don't blame them for anything, either. Simply explain your point of view, and if they aren't willing to accept it, ask them if they can leave it at that. It's good to "agree to disagree." Maintain an open dialogue where both of you can speak your minds without the fear of being attacked. If they try to manipulate you into seeing things their way, remember to stand your ground or step away from the conversation. Remember that you have a choice, whether it's deciding to agree with the other person or stick to your perspective. Standing up to a manipulator doesn't only gain you other people's respect (including theirs), but it also helps you boost your self-respect, which is one of the best things you can do for yourself.

How to Set Healthy Personal Boundaries

You can't escape manipulation if you don't have healthy personal boundaries in place. Personal boundaries are a set of rules we establish for ourselves and live in all our interactions. They help us protect ourselves and maintain our energy. Avoiding or stepping away from conversations and situations that make you feel uncomfortable, saying "no" to things that you don't feel like doing, and taking a raincheck on plans or commitments whenever you're feeling unwell are all examples of personal boundaries. These rules even guide the relationship that we have with ourselves. For instance, our personal boundaries may include refraining from negative self-talk and regularly taking time for ourselves. Boundaries are key to creating and maintaining healthy relationships.

Assume Responsibility for Your Thoughts Alone

Not everyone will agree with you or accept these changes when you introduce clear-cut boundaries in your life. This can be hard to acknowledge at first. However, you need to remind yourself that you can't change other people's thoughts and opinions. Take responsibility only for what you think and feel, and don't worry about other people.

Make Self-Care Your Priority

Think about everything that makes you feel happy, motivated, and energized, and put them into a list. Make sure to include everything that comes to your mind, no matter how small it is, such as making a stranger smile or taking a stroll in nature, to grander things like going on vacation. Make this list as long and as diverse as you can. When you're done, promise that you'll do at least one of the things on your list daily.

Trust That You Are Worthy

Even if you realize that you need to set and maintain personal boundaries, you may be subconsciously denying yourself permission to put them into practice. Perhaps you don't think you deserve to do this. Whether you're worried you might drive people away or think that you don't deserve to have rules that guide your interactions, you need to work on building up your self-compassion and self-worth. Everyone deserves to live in alignment with their beliefs and values. As odd as it sounds, it could help if you wrote up a permission slip to allow you to set up personal values in your life and put it in a place where you can always see them.

Know That It's Okay to Say "No"

There will come times when you will have to say "no" to protect yourself and maintain your personal boundaries. This can be very hard to do if you rarely turn people down. We were brought up to think that saying "no" automatically makes us disrespectful or unpleasant to be around. No one ever taught us that it's okay to say "no" whenever our own interests and mental, emotional, and physical health are in question. It's okay to say "no" even when you're not really sick or have any other convincing excuse. You can say "no" to requests simply because you don't wish to do them. It will take some practice, but it's not impossible. Soon enough, you'll realize that your true friends will not hate you or get mad at you for turning them down. The ones who do are not worth keeping around. In most cases, others will respect your choices and honesty.

Notice When You're People Pleasing

Being a people-pleaser is nothing to be ashamed of. Everyone can be a people-pleaser at times, depending on the situation or person they're dealing with. This tendency comes from a good, well-intentioned place. Everyone wishes to be liked, loved, and appreciated, and that's totally fine! People-pleasing only becomes a problem at the expense of your beliefs, values, and happiness. Not only does it tamper with your sense of identity and self-worth, but it may also lead to feelings of resentment further down the line. Prioritize your well-being and put yourself first. Everything else will come naturally, including being likable and helping others out. You can't pour from an empty cup.

Some people get anxious whenever they hear the words "personal boundaries." They think that creating boundaries for yourself causes you to shut people out. However, this is not the case. It is all about taking the time to think about what you expect from others, depending on where they stand in your life. It's about what behavior you'll never accept and from whom, and what you can afford to offer. Boundaries are one of the most significant forms of self-care. They keep you aligned with your values and help you maintain your self-respect and peace of mind. Most importantly, they allow you to fight back against manipulation and protect yourself from it.

Chapter 10

Ethical Persuasion

Ethical persuasion is a subset of influence tactics and essentially involves making logical arguments in favor of an idea, proposal, or course of action. When used ethically, these arguments are persuasive because they appeal to the other person's values and actions that are in their best interest. As such, ethical persuaders believe that their target will agree with them after hearing their logical arguments.

This chapter explains how to persuade people without exploiting them by distinguishing the differences between persuasion and manipulation. You'll also get tips on how to persuade someone to do something without adding any manipulation to it and how you can detect and prevent yourself from being manipulated.

What Is Ethical Persuasion?

When you think about persuasion, what comes to mind? Perhaps you think of salespeople persuading customers to buy their products. Or perhaps you think of unscrupulous personalities with their own form of twisted persuasion, making you question your own motivations. These are just two examples of how persuasion is used. It's a skill with its own gray area in terms of many applications and usage.

When we talk about ethical persuasion, we refer to a set of principles or standards of conduct, right and wrong, that an individual or institution believes to be universally applicable and unchangeable.

Let's use business as an example. It is not enough for them to simply sell products in today's world. Instead, organizations must also actively persuade customers to make those purchases. In other words, selling products can be an exercise in ethical persuasion. Ethical persuasion techniques are advantageous for any business or organization because these methods help them to connect with their target audience on a more personal level. When used well, this practice will lead to consumers taking action without feeling pressured or coerced. This is a very different method of persuasion from manipulation.

Essentially, it's the process of an interaction between two people where one person tries to persuade the other person to change their behavior or attitude by using ethical arguments and appealing to the correct principles or beliefs. Ethical persuasion differs from other types of persuasive techniques such as manipulation, logical or argumentative persuasion because it does not use deceptive, manipulative, or unfair tactics.

Differences between Persuasion and Manipulation

It's a natural part of human behavior to want to help others and see them succeed. This is why we often see altruistic individuals who are willing to go out of their way to help people in need. However, there are also those who take advantage of this kind of nature. Manipulation is an art form manipulators use to get what they want from others without appearing to be doing so. It's an art that involves careful planning and execution of actions designed to achieve a specific outcome. Manipulation is used by con artists, salesmen, and anyone who wants something from someone else without them realizing it.

For example, some leaders might be tempted to use manipulation techniques instead of ethical persuasion methods when it comes to business. After all, manipulation is a fast and effective way to get people to do what you want them to do. But, as any good leader knows, there's a line between using your power for good and using it for self-serving means. If you're ever in doubt about whether you should use manipulation tactics or ethical persuasion methods at work, here are some helpful tips on how you can tell the difference between the two and know which one is the right choice.

What Is Manipulation?

Manipulation is the act of controlling people or situations by deceptive or questionable means. These are usually underhanded and are meant to control a situation or person in a way that is against their best interests. Manipulative people use a variety of deceptive tactics to get you to do what they want you to do. These techniques are used to get you to do what the manipulator wants without you even realizing you've been tricked.

These are the most common manipulative techniques:

- **False Flattery:** is when someone praises you in an attempt to get you to do something for them. False flattery is often a way to get you to lower your guard and feel positive about yourself so that you're more likely to agree with them and do what they want.

- **False Urgency**: is when someone creates a false sense of urgency to get you to do what they want instantly. This can be as simple as "we need to do this right now" to more elaborate scenarios like pretending there's a major deadline that only you can meet.

- **False Promises:** are when someone makes a promise they don't intend to keep. This is often done to get you to do what they want now or in the future.

- **False Threats**: are when someone threatens you with something that's not going to happen. This is done to get you to do what they want you to do now or in the future.

Manipulation is when someone pressures you or deceives you so that they get what they want. It's not the same as persuading, influencing, or inspiring someone. Manipulative people use manipulation to get their own way, often at the expense of others. It often comes from a place of selfishness, where the manipulator doesn't care about the other person but only their own needs.

What Is Persuasion?

Persuasion is the act of influencing another person to adopt your point of view or take an action that benefits you in some way. Persuasion is often used as a marketing strategy to get customers to buy your product or service. A company might use "friendly persuasion" that feels more like a suggestion than a sales pitch or even veiled threats to convince customers.

Ethical persuasion is the art of using your communication skills and personal influence to get people to act willingly in a way that benefits your team. Ethical persuaders don't trick people into doing what they want. Instead, they guide people through logical thinking and positive emotions to get them to do what has the best overall outcome. Because it isn't about forcing people to do what you want; instead, it's about guiding people to make their own positive decisions.

These are the most common persuasive techniques:

When we deliberately try to control or influence other people's behavior to serve a purpose greater than our own, we are ethically persuasive.

- When we negotiate at a team meeting at work, we're trying to shape the outcome to benefit the department and business as a whole.

- When we try to convince a friend suffering from addiction to seek help by seeing things from our point of view, we're hoping they will change their mind to get better.

- When we cajole our children to clean their rooms, we're trying to instill a desirable trait and healthy behavior.

When a person or group is persuaded to take action or agree with your ideas, beliefs, or recommendations, they're being persuaded. It's about getting someone to do something, think a certain way, or believe something. We all have the ability to be persuasive in different situations and circumstances. With increased confidence and practice, anyone can master this skill and use it effectively in their personal and professional lives.

Essentially, manipulation and persuasion are both ways of influencing people. They just come from different intentions and have different impacts on the person being influenced.

Can You Persuade with Manipulation?

If you use manipulation to try to get what you want, you risk harming the relationship between you and the person you're trying to persuade. But if you want to be persuasive in a way that doesn't harm that relationship, you need to be genuine about it.

The good news? You don't have to be manipulative to persuade.

Manipulation requires deception and self-focus. But if you want to persuade people without feeling creepy or manipulative, you must be honest and put the other person's interests first. Manipulation is about fooling people into doing things they don't want to do. Persuasion is all about finding mutual benefit.

One way to tell if you're being either manipulative or persuasive is to ask yourself, "What do I want this person to do?" You're persuasive if you want them to do something they genuinely want to do. You're being manipulative if you want them to do something they don't want to do.

How to Persuade without Manipulation

If you want to be successful, you'll have to persuade other people to do things they might not otherwise do. But you want to do that without manipulating people and without making them feel like they've been tricked. You want them to feel like they've been treated fairly and that they're empowered to make their own decision.

Build Rapport and Trust

The easiest way to avoid manipulation is to build a friendly and trustworthy relationship with the person you want to persuade. When you build rapport, you're being authentic. You're letting your target see you and your intentions as they really are. You're not trying to fool them or hide your self-interest. You're being genuine and putting the other person's interests first.

Ask Questions and Learn Their Point of View

You can only persuade people if you know what they want and need. So the best way to persuade people is to ask them what they want. Don't assume you know what they want. Let them tell you.

Communicate Your Needs

Self-advocacy is making a case for yourself by describing your personal experiences. Self-advocacy is often used when a person needs something that may be difficult to obtain. For example, a student may ask their professor to extend a deadline. It can take different forms, including storytelling, outlining your strengths and weaknesses, and describing your needs. When using self-advocacy, you should start by explaining the situation, providing context, and then communicating how you want the situation to be resolved.

Offer Fair Value in Exchange for What You Want

If you want to persuade people to do something, you must give them something in exchange. If you want to get someone to do something, make a genuine request. Instead of trying to trick them into doing it, let them know why you want them to do it and how it will benefit them. Let them know what's in it for them, and show them that you truly care about their needs and wants.

Get to Know Your Audience

If you want to get someone to agree with you, do some research into their beliefs. You'll want to ensure that your ideas fit in with their beliefs and values.

Have Principles

Principled persuasion is a method that puts forward an idea by appealing to values and common sense. It can be used to make a case for a particular idea, course of action, or policy proposal. When using this technique, you can explain why a particular idea is important, identify the values at stake, and then propose a course of action that is consistent with those values.

Be Open to Others

Manipulative people often try to convince you that they are right and you are wrong. Instead of trying to make someone feel bad for disagreeing with you, let them know that you respect their right to have a different opinion. Be willing to discuss your ideas with them and acknowledge that they may also have some valid points.

Do You Really Care?

Suppose you want to be more persuasive without manipulation. In that case, you'll need to ensure that you are genuinely interested in the needs and desires of the people you are trying to persuade. You'll need to show that you care about their interests and goals.

Be Respectful

If you want people to listen to you, you need to make sure that they feel you respect them and are genuinely interested in what they have to say. You can't expect people to respect your input if you aren't respecting their thoughts and beliefs. If you don't respect other people's opinions, you can't expect them to listen to you or take your input seriously.

Recognize Them as Real People

The recognition method is a technique that presents an idea and appeals to the other person's past experiences and successes. You can use the recognition method to make a case for a particular idea by describing how your idea will allow others to build on their strengths and past successes. You can use the recognition method in various situations, including negotiations, problem-solving, and decision-making.

Worldwide Ethics of Persuasion and Manipulation

If you've ever found yourself in the middle of an argument, you probably know how tough it can be to come to a mutually agreeable resolution. Unless both parties are willing to put their egos aside and find common ground, any sort of resolution is almost impossible.

Or is it? Sometimes, successfully resolving an argument isn't necessarily about finding a solution that makes everybody happy. Instead, it's about finding a solution that doesn't necessarily win the argument but wins the person. In ethical persuasion, logic is used to make a case for an idea, proposal, or course of action. These arguments are persuasive when used ethically because they appeal to the other person's values and actions that work in their best interests. Because of this, ethical persuaders anticipate their target's agreement after hearing their logical arguments.

How to Tell the Difference between Manipulation and Ethical Persuasion

Manipulators will often take you off guard by quickly trying to get what they want with false urgency. They want to convince you to do what they want now, immediately. On the other hand, ethical persuaders will be patient and willing to walk you through the logical reasons why you should go along with their plan. Ethical persuaders will also be willing to take as much time as needed to determine whether their plan is even the right one, to begin with.

Manipulators will often use false flattery to get what they want from you. They will compliment you on making you feel good about yourself and make you more likely to agree with them. Ethical persuaders, on the other hand, will often praise you for who you are and what you do.

Manipulators will often make false promises to get what they want from you. They will promise you something but have no intention of ever delivering it. On the other hand, ethical persuaders will make positive promises and be fully committed to fulfilling them.

Manipulators will often make false threats to get what they want from you. They will threaten you with something that isn't actually going to happen. On the other hand, ethical persuaders will only threaten you if they are fully committed to following through on that threat.

Why Use Ethical Persuasion?

Like all forms of communication, persuasion can be used for good or for bad. But, ethical persuasion is a powerful way to help others understand your message and take action for social good. It can be used to change hearts, minds, and actions for the better.

For example, ethical persuasion can be used to help:

- Educate others on critical issues and create conversations around solutions.

- Raise awareness, inspire action, and create social change.

- Change policies and laws.

- Energize communities to take action.

- Accelerate social impact.

Persuasion in the World: How Does It Work?

Ethical persuasion works because it helps others understand the importance of an issue and a solution. It helps people connect the dots to understand how an issue impacts them personally and why acting on it is important.

- It helps others see the relevance of an issue and solution.

- It helps others understand how they are impacted.

- It helps others feel engaged in solving the issue.

To do this, you need to understand the issue you're promoting and the people you're trying to reach. You need to know what others are thinking and feeling about the issue so that you can engage their emotions and connect their hearts to the issue.

- You need to understand the issue and why it's important.

- You need to know the people you're trying to reach and speak to them in a language they understand.

- You need to understand what others are thinking and feeling about the issue

It is possible to become more persuasive without manipulating others, but it takes some effort. If you manipulate people, you can't expect them to listen to you or even want to work with you. People won't respect your input or suggestions if you aren't genuinely interested in their views or make them feel like they are wrong. You have to be willing to listen to their ideas and suggestions and be honest and authentic. If you are willing to make changes and compromise, you will find that people are willing to work with you and accept your ideas.

Luckily, there are ways to achieve this. Ethical persuasion is a powerful tool to change hearts, minds, and actions for the better. You can use it to raise awareness, inspire action, and create social change. In addition to changing policies and laws, it can energize communities and accelerate social impact. When done right, ethical persuasion can be an invaluable tool for those who work for the social good.

Conclusion

This comprehensive beginner's guide was written to explain and give readers in-depth information on effective techniques to influence human behavior and help them master dark psychology and manipulation. It offers tips that can be used by people to protect themselves from the practice of dark psychology and gaslighting manipulation.

Each chapter deals with a different facet of these intriguing subjects. The first chapter explains the meaning of persuasion and when and why it is used. It also explains how persuasion is used and how it affects the people being persuaded. The chapter also explains its benefits.

In the second chapter, we delved into persuasion techniques and explained how each method is used. The common techniques include the usage of force, creating a need, persuasion, utilizing illustrative words, and tricks used by mass media. We dedicated the third chapter to manipulation techniques commonly used, such as mind control. We explained how mind control is used, how it affects the individuals being persuaded, and the benefits of using this technique.

Chapter four focused on explaining different mind control techniques. These techniques include brainwashing, repetition, hypnosis, power, propaganda, conversion techniques, and persuading with willpower. Gaslighting is another technique used to manipulate others, and we explained the meaning of this concept in chapter five. We explained how it is done and affects the individuals being persuaded as well as the benefits.

Chapter six outlines the traits of gaslighters and how they use them to manipulate others. These traits include lying, refusing to admit flaws, exaggerating, false image projection, becoming aggressive when persuaded, and violating boundaries. Gaslighters also use coercion, emotional validation, and controlling others. We also explained how these traits are used to harm others.

In chapter seven, we explained the methods used by gaslighters to control others to do what they want. In chapter eight, we discussed the methods you can take to avoid gaslighting. It also covered the effects of gaslighting and how they can affect the reader. We provided the methods that can be used to set boundaries and stop gaslighters.

In chapter nine, we explained the methods that can be used to escape from manipulation and dark psychology. The techniques you can use include setting boundaries, observing people, countering the gaslighter's demands, knowing what you want, saying no, standing for yourself, and rethinking everything you're asked to do.

Finally, we explained how you could persuade people without manipulating them. The differences between manipulation and persuasion are highlighted in this section. We provided details about the measures you can take to persuade someone without crossing their boundaries.

Thank you for buying and reading/listening to our book. If you found this book useful/helpful please take a few minutes and leave a review on Amazon.com or Audible.com (if you bought the audio version).

References

Jones, M. B. (2016, October 12). How to be Persuasive, and Why Every Type of Professional Needs This Skill. Pcc.Edu. https://climb.pcc.edu/blog/how-to-be-persuasive-and-why-every-type-of-professional-needs-this-skill

The Benefits of Effective Influencing Skills. (2011, October 13). Small Business - Chron.Com. https://smallbusiness.chron.com/benefits-effective-influencing-skills-31374.html

Cherry, K. (n.d.). What Is Persuasion? Verywell Mind. https://www.verywellmind.com/what-is-persuasion-2795892

Doyle, A. (n.d.). What Is Persuasion? The Balance Careers. https://www.thebalancecareers.com/persuasive-skills-with-examples-2059694

What Is Persuasion? Definition, Examples, and How It Works. (n.d.). Indeed Career Guide. https://in.indeed.com/career-advice/career-development/what-is-persuasion

McShane, R. (2021, December 14). How Persuasion Skills Can Benefit Your Career. Wharton Online. https://online.wharton.upenn.edu/blog/how-persuasion-skills-can-benefit-your-career/

Persuasion, Attitudes, & Social Cognition. (n.d.). Upenn.Edu. https://www.asc.upenn.edu/research/centers/social-action-lab/research/persuasion-attitudes-and-social-cognition

Persuasion and Influence: Definitions, Benefits and Tips. (n.d.). Indeed Career Guide. https://www.indeed.com/career-advice/career-development/persuasion-and-influence

Aaftink, M. (2017, September 12). The 10 most common used persuasion techniques in marketing campaigns. Digital Movers B.V. https://digitalmovers.nl/the-10-most-common-used-persuasion-techniques-in-marketing-campaigns/

Methods of Persuasion. (n.d.). Ripon College https://ripon.edu/methods-of-persuasion/

Cherry, K. (n.d.). A Quick Guide to Becoming a Master of Persuasion. Verywell Mind. https://www.verywellmind.com/how-to-become-a-master-of-persuasion-2795901

6 Types of Persuasion. (2011, August 24). Synonym.Com. https://classroom.synonym.com/6-types-persuasion-12004696.html

Medaglia, J. D., Zurn, P., Sinnott-Armstrong, W., & Bassett, D. S. (2017). Mind control as a guide for the mind. Nature Human Behaviour, 1(6), 0119. https://doi.org/10.1038/s41562-017-0119

Sharie Stines, L. (2019, March 15). Understanding Manipulative Mind Control and What to do About It (Part 1). Psych Central. https://psychcentral.com/pro/recovery-expert/2019/03/understanding-manipulative-mind-control-and-what-to-do-about-it-part-1

Morrow, J. (2011, August 25). A 7-Step Guide to Mind Control: How to Quit Begging and Make People *Want* to Help You. Copyblogger. https://copyblogger.com/mind-control-marketing/

Huang, L., & Yu, R. (2020, July 31). How to (Actually) Change Someone's Mind. Harvard Business Review. https://hbr.org/2020/07/how-to-actually-change-someones-mind

Douglas Fields, R. (n.d.). Mind Reading and Mind Control Technologies Are Coming. Scientific American Blog Network https://blogs.scientificamerican.com/observations/mind-reading-and-mind-control-technologies-are-coming/

J. K. Ellis, D. J. (2011). Mind Control 101 - How to Influence the Thoughts and Actions of Others Without Them Knowing Or Caring. Lulu.com.

Mind Control. (n.d.). Changingminds.Org http://changingminds.org/techniques/mind_control/mind_control.htm

Mind Control Techniques To Be Aware Of. (n.d.). Psychologia.Co https://psychologia.co/mind-control-techniques/

Layton, J., & Hoyt, A. (2006, May 10). How Brainwashing Works. HowStuffWorks. https://science.howstuffworks.com/life/inside-the-mind/human-brain/brainwashing.htm

Is Total Mind Control Possible? (n.d.). Psychology Today https://www.psychologytoday.com/us/blog/hypnosis-the-power-trance/201509/is-total-mind-control-possible

Lim, S. (2019, January 2). Hypnosis: Mind Control? Linkedin.Com; LinkedIn. https://www.linkedin.com/pulse/hypnosis-mind-control-sylvester-lim

7 signs of gaslighting at the workplace. (n.d.). Psychology Today. https://www.psychologytoday.com/us/blog/communication-success/202007/7-signs-gaslighting-the-workplace

Are gaslighters aware of what they do? (n.d.). Psychology Today. https://www.psychologytoday.com/us/blog/here-there-and-everywhere/201701/are-gaslighters-aware-what-they-do

Conrad, M. (2021, June 22). What is gaslighting? Meaning, examples and support. Forbes. https://www.forbes.com/health/mind/what-is-gaslighting/

DiGiulio, S. (2018, July 13). What is gaslighting? And how do you know if it's happening to you? NBC News. https://www.nbcnews.com/better/health/what-gaslighting-how-do-you-know-if-it-s-happening-ncna890866

Gordon, S. (2017, August 1). What Is Gaslighting? Verywell Mind. https://www.verywellmind.com/is-someone-gaslighting-you-4147470

Hoare, K. (2021, September 6). What is media gaslighting? Happiful Magazine. https://happiful.com/what-is-media-gaslighting/

Holland, B. (2021, September 2). For those who experience gaslighting, the widespread misuse of the word is damaging. Well+Good. https://www.wellandgood.com/misuse-gaslighting/

How gaslighting in marketing will damage your business. (n.d.). Bragg Media Marketing https://braggmedia.com/gaslighting-in-marketing/

Huizen, J. (2022, July 14). What is gaslighting? Medicalnewstoday.com. https://www.medicalnewstoday.com/articles/gaslighting

Lindsay, J. (2018, April 5). What is gaslighting? The meaning and origin of the term explained. Metro.co.uk. https://metro.co.uk/2018/04/05/what-is-gaslighting-7443188/

Morris, S. Y., & Raypole, C. (2021, November 24). Gaslighting: Signs and tips for seeking help. Healthline. https://www.healthline.com/health/gaslighting

Nall, R., MSN, & CRNA. (2020, June 29). Gaslighting: What it is, long-term effects, and what to do. Medicalnewstoday.com. https://www.medicalnewstoday.com/articles/long-term-effects-of-gaslighting

www.ingramcontent.com/pod-product-compliance
Lightning Source LLC
LaVergne TN
LVHW020715160325
806028LV00010B/539